Staying Away from the Edge

Robyn Mulder

STAYING AWAY FROM THE EDGE

Published by Start Living Press.

Photo of the Grand Canyon taken by Gary Mulder
Front cover design: Cathy Rueter
Back cover and interior formatting: Robyn Mulder

ISBN: 979-8-9900920-0-6 (paperback)
ISBN: 979-8-9900920-1-3 (e-book)

To Gary

Thanks for sticking with me through all of the ups and downs of depression and anxiety. As much as I resisted, I'm glad you never stopped encouraging me to "write the book."

And some notes of thanks

Thank you to every person who supported me as I went through the crisis I refer to in this book. I don't want to single anyone out (heaven forbid I should forget anyone), but you know who you are. I'm grateful for the encouragement, help, and support I received from each of you as I made it through that depressive episode.

I'd also like to thank everyone who helped me as I worked on writing this book. It took way too many years, but I have to trust that God's timing is perfect and this is the right time for it to be published. I know so many of you are saying, "It's about time!" Thank you for your words of advice and for cheering me on every step of the way.

Contents

The Story Behind the Title

Written by my husband, Gary Mulder, 2015

So, we're staying at my in-laws . . . sleeping on an air mattress . . . gently rolling around as one is prone to do in the early morning. Suddenly, I hear the beginnings of a scream. I feel a moment of sheer panic and confusion. What is going on? After what seems like an eternity, I feel a hard thud and my wife is lying on the floor.

I can barely hold it in. *Stifle it. Don't let it out. She's not going to think this is funny*. But it is! She just fell out of bed. I lie there trying to feign compassion, trying not to let the vibrations of my muffled belly laugh shake the air mattress, which will give away the fact that I think this is all way too hilarious.

It's good to be able to laugh again. It's been a while since laughter filled our house. Depression is like that. It robs you of the joys of life. It takes away the good times. Nothing seems fun or happy or worth sharing. It isolates and destroys what should be a happy life together.

My wife had just gone through a severe bout of depression, but that's her story to tell. I merely went along for the ride. Because that's what spouses do. We experience it from the other side.

After this incident happened, sleep was out of the question. I had to get up and write down my thoughts.

I returned to the scene of the crash to find my wife perfectly centered on the air mattress. As I gently tried to wriggle my way back in and onto my side, I asked, "What are you doing way over here?" Her bleary-eyed response: "I'm staying away from the edge . . ."

Depression is a little like dozing in that sleeping bag on a two-foot-tall air mattress. Your slumber becomes rather restless at first. You gently roll to the side. You struggle to get comfortable, but nothing works. Then, all of a sudden, you feel that moment of panic when you know something is wrong.

You scream . . . but the scream is not loud or intense enough to muster any real help. Your hands and feet are bound in the sleeping bag, so you're helpless as you slide over the edge. Falling . . . falling . . . falling . . . and a thud at the bottom.

Your loved one witnesses your plight, but they are bound in their own figurative sleeping bag. They know you're in trouble. They want to help. But it's too late. The fall has already begun. It's just a matter of time before they hear you hit the bottom.

This book is about "staying away from the edge." It's a chronicle of hope and help and healing. It's a journey toward wholeness . . . a search for more joy in life . . . a path for those still dealing with depression.

As you read *Staying Away from the Edge*, I hope you apply the principles to your own journey toward joy. It is an honest depiction of life after my wife's depression, the struggles that landed her there, and the hope that lies ahead for anyone who struggles with this issue.

—Pastor Gary Mulder

As We Begin

The book you are about to read is based on my personal experience with anxiety and depression. Certain things I share may be triggers if you also deal with any type of mental illness. I am not a trained counselor or therapist. I'm sharing my story to encourage and inspire you to take the steps appropriate for you to get to better emotional health. That will look different for each person.

I urge you to stop reading and reach out for help if you find yourself feeling more anxious and hopeless as you go through this book. Talk to a family member or friend, call your doctor or therapist, or call the 988 Suicide & Crisis Lifeline if life just seems too overwhelming.

Mental illness is treatable. You don't have to suffer alone. There is help. There is hope. But you have to let someone know how you're feeling.

Praying for you,

~Robyn

Part 1:
Over the Edge

Chapter 1

How Did I Get Here?

The cords of death entangled me, the anguish of the grave came over me; I was overcome by distress and sorrow. (Psalm 116:3 NIV)

I grasped the cold plastic cord with shaking hands and pulled a little tighter. I looked around the dark basement desperately. Old cans of paint, piles of camping gear packed away for another season, the half-finished dollhouse. Nothing offered relief from the pain. My mind still churned. I still wanted out. To be done. With life. With everything.

Should I pull until I couldn't breathe? Would that do it? My husband was busy at church. Our girls were away at college. Our boys were occupied upstairs with homework or video games. No one would find me for a while.

But someone would find me. Dead, or just unconscious, *someone* in my family would have to go through the shock and pain of finding me like this.

I unwrapped the extension cord from my neck and threw it on the floor in disgust and horror. I moaned in frustration, then clamped trembling fingers over my mouth.

I glanced at the orange pile tangled at my feet and watched as teardrops plopped among the loops. Hopeless. Again. But I didn't want to kill myself. Did I?

What was I doing?

How did I get here?

***

I don't want to write this book.

I want it to be written, of course, but *I* don't want to write it.

I don't want to think about the ups and downs of anxiety and depression.

I don't want to relive the confusing, desperate feelings of the darkest place I've ever been.

I don't want to think about the fear and pain I put my family and friends through.

I don't want to admit that my thoughts still push and pull me in that direction sometimes. I wonder if I'll be able to turn it around and get healthy again.

But then . . .

Then . . . the daughter of a friend dies by suicide after a long battle with depression.

Then . . . someone asks if I think they should get professional help for the anxiety they're feeling. They're not sure if it's clinical or if they can just get through it on their own.

Then . . . tears well up in the eyes of a friend whose husband died nearly a year ago. She's struggling, trying to cope with the loss.

Then . . . the daughter of another dear friend dies by suicide with no warning. The only thing her dad could find was a reference in this sixteen-year-old's journal saying nobody cared. So many people did. How could this have happened?

Then I know I must write this book. Even though there are other books out there about mental illness, I need to add *my* story. Someone out there (maybe you?) needs to know there is help and hope after you've been diagnosed. There are things you can do to stay healthy and live a fulfilling life, even when the symptoms of your illness flare up.

THERE IS HOPE

I didn't plan to go over the edge. No one ever does, I suppose, and yet our mental health system is full of people who have done just that. An out-of-control addiction to drugs or alcohol, the tragedy of losing a loved one, the end of a marriage. What sent me over the edge? A teaching job.

Yes, you read that right. A high school teaching job brought me to such hopelessness that I considered taking my own life.

Now, before you throw this book down in disbelief (*What does this woman know about the pain I feel?*), I urge you to stay with me. I know that teaching may seem like a minor problem compared to what you have gone through. Maybe you've had major health concerns or someone you love has died. Maybe you've experienced years of abuse or you're dealing with financial burdens that seem insurmountable.

It really doesn't matter *what* our individual situations are. The fact is that *something* changes our brain chemistry and starts us on a long spiral into anxiety and depression. We can't compare our situation to anyone else's. Truth is, some people can make it through demanding times without getting sick. They seem to have a well of optimism that never runs dry. Others (maybe that's you and me) are blessed with a mind that thinks a little too much, focuses on the negative, and eventually wants to throw in the proverbial towel. If we aren't careful, our broken brains can send us right over the edge.

It doesn't matter how or why, but I've been there. Try not to get hung up on what sent *me* over the edge. Instead, try to apply the things you read here to your own life situation, whatever that may be.

I've learned some things over the years. The book you hold in your hands is proof that it's possible to push past our insecurities and live well in spite of a mental health diagnosis.

Life isn't perfect. I still feel hopeless at times. But it never gets as bad as it did in 2014, and those feelings never last as long as they did back then.

There is hope. For me and for you.

WHAT TO EXPECT IN THIS BOOK

In the preface ("The Story Behind the Title"), you heard from my husband, Pastor Gary Mulder, who watched helplessly as I bounced through the highs and lows of life, finally careening over the edge just a month into the teaching job. In the rest of this book, we'll explore what it's like to go over the edge, how we even get close to it in the first place, and how we can stay away from that dangerous drop-off.

My faith in God is vital to me. In some ways, that may have contributed to the anxiety and depression, but it was also a lifeline when it felt like all hope was gone. Even if you don't share my beliefs, I encourage you to keep reading. I'm pretty sure you'll find something helpful.

Your journey may not look exactly like mine, but I'm willing to bet we have some things in common. Together, we can explore our illnesses and things to do as we move ahead in life.

Let's start at the scariest place: over the edge itself.

***

Muffled screams came from behind the locked door. Staff rushed to the area. I couldn't see what was happening, but what I heard was unsettling. The other patients didn't appear to be upset.

How did I get here? I didn't belong in a mental health unit, did I? When I arrived, one of the patients asked me if I was from Pharmacy because I was wearing scrubs from the hospital across town. "No, she's a patient," one of the nurses explained before she got me some new garments.

I was embarrassed, but also relieved that I didn't *look* like I belonged here. But I did. I really did.

It didn't matter that I was a 48-year-old pastor's wife with four children and a good job. It didn't matter that I was a college-educated Christian with loving family members and friends.

I was in the hospital because I had lost all hope and wanted to die. The patients around me were in the same boat. We all had a mental health crisis that sent us over the edge.

My hopelessness had led to a cord around my neck, a drastic decision even though I hadn't pulled it tight. The other patients had chosen a variety of ways to show their despair: overdosing, throwing themselves in front of a moving vehicle, or some other method they weren't willing to share.

In the safety of the hospital, we could look at our situations objectively, calmly even.

The hospital was such a contrast to what I was used to. I had never heard people talking about the disturbing symptoms of their mental illness. I was surprised to hear people comparing different mental health units around the state, listing the pros and cons of each from their personal experiences. I hadn't known too many people covered in tattoos, but I saw plenty of that here—even on one man's eyelids. When I noticed them during one of our mealtimes and asked about it, he calmly closed his eyes and I saw the message "F*%k Off." He opened his eyes and grinned.

Really, what was I doing here?

WHAT DOES IT ALL MEAN?

Before we go any further, let me be clear on what it means to me to go *over the edge*. Some people may think that going "over the edge" means dying by suicide. That's not how I'm defining it.

People use a variety of phrases to describe when someone reaches a point of emotional crisis: *They went crazy. She went off the deep end. They're psychotic. He had a nervous breakdown.*

Let's take a look at that last one, because it's still used quite often to describe someone's situation, even though the term is no longer used by mental health professionals today.

In an article at mayoclinic.org, Daniel K. Hall-Flavin, M.D. explains: "*Nervous breakdown* is sometimes used by people to describe a stressful situation in which they're temporarily unable to function normally in day-to-day life. It's commonly understood to occur when life's demands become physically and emotionally overwhelming."[1]

In my opinion, this is what it comes down to when I talk about going *over the edge*. A person's ability to function is in jeopardy and they get to the point where they can no longer ignore their symptoms. They need to do something to end the stress, pain, and hopelessness they're feeling.

Going over the edge can look different for everyone. For some people, a hospital visit isn't necessary. They just reach a crisis point and need to withdraw from their job, school, or other outside responsibilities while they recover.

Some may go over the edge and attempt to die by suicide. Others get to the point where they are thinking about death and other catastrophic thoughts all the time, making them incapable of functioning and fulfilling their daily tasks. Some people get angry and violent, wanting to lash out and hurt those around them because of the pain they feel inside. They might decide to seek help on their own or be forced to get counseling when they act out and commit a crime.

---

1   https://www.mayoclinic.org/diseases-conditions/depression/expert-answers/nervous-breakdown/faq-20057830

Is there shame in this illness? There shouldn't be, but there often is. Many people don't tell others that they even got sick—let alone went to a hospital—because they're embarrassed. They suffer alone with their emotions, or they come home from a hospital stay to the same stresses and problems. Because of their silence, they don't have the support they need.

If they aren't careful, they could end up right back where they started. Their lack of hope could cause them to be isolated at home or put them back in the hospital.

The Merriam-Webster Dictionary defines it like this:

over the edge: into a mental or emotional state that makes someone completely lose control. Example: His friends worried that the news might send/drive/push him *over the edge*.[2]

That's how I'm using the term "over the edge" in this book. I see it as someone getting so ill that they lose control. They run out of hope. They can't function. Those of us that go this route may withdraw from our schools, jobs, and social lives, hiding under the covers because we can't cope. Or we may soldier on through the pain, showing up for all our obligations in spite of

---

2   Merriam-Webster.com, s.v. "over the edge," https://www. merriam-webster.com/dictionary/over%20the%20edge.

the feelings inside. We may have suicidal thoughts that either scare us into getting help or make us hide further.

Someone who goes over the edge may eventually attempt suicide, possibly ending their life if they aren't rescued from that attempt.

Whatever the case, the person has essentially gone over the edge. If they survive the crisis, they must try to go back to their normal daily life. Now begins the long road of recovery.

SO MANY QUESTIONS

I wonder, did I actually attempt suicide? I had an extension cord around my neck. Is that any different than trying to swallow a handful of pills, or cutting, or any one of the other things we hear about? It's all a cry for help from our hurt. I maintained enough control that I removed the cord from my neck and went back to my schoolwork, even though I was shaking, tearful, and anxious.

The fact that I felt such hopelessness and picked up the cord in my desperation is close enough. Maybe we can agree that I went "over the edge" even though I didn't lose complete control.

That's part of the problem. There are so many degrees of "over the edge" and depths to which people plummet within any mental illness.

For some people it might be like falling into a deep grassy ditch, for others it could be like bouncing down from a fifty-foot cliff, and for too many it could be like hurtling to a painful death in the Grand Canyon.

IT'S WORTH TRYING

Who am I to suggest that you can get better? Is it arrogant to assume anyone can actually stay away from the edge when they are diagnosed with a mental illness? Is it cruel to offer hope to you if you've struggled with mental illness for years and years, making you think you can live a better life? Will this book just be a slap in the face for those who continue in recurring cycles of depression? Will it be an unwanted reminder that some people live good, fulfilling, thriving lives while they themselves are stuck over the edge with few expectations of getting better?

That's such a tough question. After pondering this for many years, my conclusion is that it's always worth trying. Of course there are going to be people who continue to struggle with their mental health because of life situations and the chemical imbalances that occur in their brains. But if certain symptoms could improve because of better thinking, medication, and/or talking through situations with a therapist, isn't that worth the effort?

It's so difficult. When we are well, it's easy to look at the person who can't get out of bed and say, "Well, just get up!"

And, honestly, we probably could feel better—most of the time—if we got out of bed even when we didn't feel like it. Getting our actions and thoughts going in a forward direction can lead to more positive ways of thinking, feeling, and acting, while wallowing in negative thoughts can move our lives in ways that lead to horrible thoughts, feelings, and actions. But a person in crisis can't see that.

So, when we're the ones who are healthy, there are questions for us as well: What is the answer? How much do we push people to get better? How much do we allow them to stay in bed, hide from social interaction, and withdraw from society?

I could say, "It's all too hard! I might as well not even write a book on this topic because it's just going to offend people."

But what about the people it could help? (I'm praying that's you, dear reader.) What about the people who are struggling greatly but could get to a better place with a little direction? What about the people that have felt the depths of hopelessness but have the ability to practice better thinking—taking action steps to get healthy again and thrive in life—even if they wobble a bit once in a while and slip back into depression?

I can't claim that I have an answer for everyone struggling with a mental illness. But that doesn't mean I should be silent. Perhaps something I share can be helpful. Maybe something you read will improve some aspect of your life—no matter what level of mental illness affects you.

As we get started, it might be helpful to compare mental illness to a physical injury or illness.

BROKEN IS BROKEN

Once in a while, people break their arm or leg. We would never think of saying to someone: "Use that broken arm to lift those boxes!" or "Just get up and walk on that broken leg!" When a limb is fractured, we know it needs to be set and then it needs to rest for a certain number of weeks or months as it heals.

When the proper amount of time has passed, that person goes to physical therapy. They start to use their arm or leg again, even if it's awkward or painful. Eventually, they get to the point where they're using it completely. Sometimes they heal up as good as new, but other times they might retain a slight limp or something that hinders them from being fully what they were before.

OUT OF COMMISSION

If someone has a physical illness, there is often a point of crisis where they are incapacitated for a time. They lie in the hospital bed, hooked up to IVs administering antibiotics or another medicine that combats the illness racking the person's body. Once the illness runs its course, the IV is removed and the person goes home. A recovery period is usually needed, but eventually the person gets to a stable place where they can function again. Sometimes they can function just like before, but sometimes there are lingering effects of the illness.

PROGRESSIVE DISEASES

Sometimes a person gets a condition that progresses over the years until they finally pass away when the illness takes over their entire system. Infirmities like cerebral palsy, ALS (formerly known as Lou Gehrig's Disease), muscular dystrophy, and Alzheimer's can present a variety of symptoms that are annoyances at first. Gradually the nerves, muscles, or memories break down until normal functioning is no longer possible. Doctors and other health professionals do everything they can to slow the progression of the disease, but little can be done to stop what's happening to the body or brain.

WHERE DOES MENTAL ILLNESS FIT?

So, where does mental health fit into these categories? Maybe it can be all three.

Sometimes a person has a mental health crisis and it's like a broken leg. It happens all at once, the person needs to stay at home and get treatment for the crisis, but after a few months they have healed. They take medicine and undergo therapy and they go back to life as normal. After a time, they may even be able to drop the medicine and stop seeing the therapist. They're healed and they probably won't get sick again.

Sometimes the emotional disorder is like an illness that hits suddenly, and the person is incapacitated for a time. They go to the hospital, get medicine, talk to doctors and therapists, and stay there until the crisis has passed. When they are in a more stable place, they go home and continue the medicine and therapy until they get well enough to discontinue those things.

Sometimes a person becomes mentally ill and the rest of their life is a slow decline (or an attempt at maintenance) until they die. They need to go on disability They can never get off their medicine. They will always need to talk to a therapist. A full recovery won't happen because it's just not possible.

Just because there are people out there who may never recover fully from a mental illness doesn't mean this book shouldn't be written. We don't refuse to treat someone with a broken leg just because there is another person out there who has a degenerative disease who will keep wasting away indefinitely. No, we prescribe amoxicillin and other antibiotics for people suffering from an infection. We put casts on people's broken arms and legs. We let people rest and eat chicken noodle soup when they're sick—and take a couple of days off work. We help them even though there are other people in the process of dying and dealing with all the pain and heartache that their own disease brings.

NO MIRACLE CURES

I know you might be hoping that this book will be the answer you've been looking for as you deal with your mental illness.

Sorry to disappoint you, but I can't promise you a miracle cure. I don't know where you're at emotionally. This is just my story. Each person's illness is different. This book won't solve all your problems, but it may give you some good tools to use as you work toward better mental health.

You may make it through a time of crisis and get back to great emotional health, not needing medication or ongoing counseling. You may pull through the crisis and learn to live life well as you continue to deal with symptoms, utilizing medications and t h e r a p y to stay healthy. You may survive a crisis, but still be plagued with intense symptoms that hang on despite meds and talk therapy.

Each of those scenarios is going to take some work on your part to stay healthy and not succumb to mental illness.

We'll explore what that looks like in the rest of this book. I'll share some things I've learned over the years, but there is a world of information out there. We each need to keep searching until we find what works for us.

Being in the mental health unit back in 2014 was good for me in so many ways. In group counseling sessions, I learned that everyone there had flawed ways of dealing with life situations, whether those experiences were traumatic or rather mundane. Each of us went over the edge because we got sicker and sicker but hadn't taken the actions necessary to stop the downward spiral before it ended in total despair. We found ourselves in the hospital, whether we felt like we belonged there or not, because we had gone over the edge.

The question remains—how *did* we get there? Was there any way we could have avoided that circumstance?

Our individual situations were vastly different, but there was one thing we all *could* have done to at least decrease the likelihood of going over the edge, but we didn't.

First, we had to admit there was a problem.

Staying Away from the Edge Takeaways

- 🎵 There is hope (even if you don't feel it).

- 🎵 Going over the edge can look different for every person, but it basically means you've lost the ability to function in day-to-day life.

- 🎵 Isolation and shame can keep us stuck in the downward spiral of mental illness.

- 🎵 It's worth trying to get well again (whether your illness is a one-time event, a longer situation, or a life-long progression).

- 🎵 The first step is admitting there is a problem.

Chapter 2

Admitting There Is a Problem

Then they cried out to the LORD in their trouble, and he delivered them from their distress. (Psalm 107:6 NIV)

I sat fidgeting at my desk during my planning period at school. I jumped as the door between my classroom and the adjacent room opened and the science teacher came in. She had been good friends with the previous Spanish teacher and had gotten used to using this shortcut on her way to the staff room and office. She must have noticed the stressed look on my face because she paused before she got to the main door. "You know," she observed, "I can see that you're struggling, but I don't know what to do to help."

"I'm okay," I squeaked. "It will get better."

"Well, if there's anything you need help with, just let me know," she offered as she went on her way.

I had just lied to someone who was offering to help me. I *wasn't* okay. I needed help with so many things. I needed help figuring out the online gradebook and other technology troubles that were stressing me out. I needed to share what I was feeling about the discipline problems I was having and get some ideas for how to handle disruptions in the classroom. I knew I needed help in all those areas, but I wasn't willing to ask for it. I didn't really want to admit there was a problem.

My thoughts bounced back and forth between "I'm smart. I just need to give myself some time. I can do this!" and "Aaaah! What am I doing? This is so hard! What's wrong with me?" Over time, that second group of thoughts became more and more frequent, and the first set got squashed until I could barely think them anymore.

I continued to spiral down because I refused to admit there was any kind of problem. It was amazing how quickly it happened as I look back on it all these years later.

EXCITING SUMMER TURNS TO FALL FIASCO

During the summer of 2011, I felt a little nervous, but I attributed it to excitement for the new job. I was sure I was going to be a great teacher. I would be Señora M—the cool teacher with just an initial for her name.

We would sing Spanish songs with my guitar, do crafts, watch movies, and have fun learning to speak Spanish.

I poured myself into researching a new method for teaching foreign languages called TPRS (Teaching Proficiency through Reading and Storytelling). Instead of just memorizing vocabulary and reciting different verb forms, the teacher uses stories to get the students immersed in the language. Kids have fun as they absorb the language. All the videos I watched and books I read showed awesome results and students who *loved* their language classes.

When the school year began, I used the new method with the Spanish 1 and 2 classes, while sticking to a more traditional approach in Spanish 3 and 4.

Good things were happening in all the classes at first, but bad things started happening inside of me. I put so much pressure on myself to do well, and I just couldn't keep up. I was hyper-focused on each and every student's facial expression. If they looked bored, I figured it was my fault. If they seemed frustrated or confused, I blamed myself.

I remembered the boredom, frustration, and confusion of high school as a teenager. As a student, I never gave my teachers much thought. The classes were mandatory and it sure wasn't *their* fault if I was bored or frustrated (well, maybe sometimes it *was* their fault, but I wasn't blaming them as a teenager).

I had seen those looks over twenty years earlier when I taught full-time after college. As the teacher, I noticed my students' feelings, but I had the energy and dedication to teach for two years.

I saw them again as a sub in the school system for several years. As a substitute teacher, I could refer students back to their regular teachers and let them deal with it.

Now I had my own classroom again and those looks really bothered me. I didn't have the energy I could draw on in my twenties, and the stress soon caught up with me.

I started to feel an almost constant ache in my stomach. I had to use the bathroom before school started and often throughout the day. I began to lose weight because I just had no appetite. I had a hard time concentrating and I couldn't relax. I was constantly analyzing how I was doing. Was the new method working? Could the students tell how nervous I was?

I worried about how my students were doing. I couldn't enjoy the thrill that many of them expressed as they learned new words and began communicating in Spanish. I was fixated on what I could do to change the minds of the kids who entered the room, plopped down into their seats, and announced daily, "I hate Spanish!"

I wondered what the other teachers thought of me. In staff meetings and at lunch, I stayed pretty quiet, afraid to voice the thoughts running through my head. One day two teachers invited me to eat with them in the home economics room. I was shocked when the conversation turned to a student whose father had died by suicide the year before. The women remarked about how badly that had affected the man's family, completely unaware that similar thoughts were flitting through my mind increasingly more often. I said nothing about how I was feeling, of course.

I marveled at how relaxed the other teachers seemed to be as we interacted each day. Even when one of them admitted he had struggled at first, I could only despair over the fact that he said he hadn't felt comfortable teaching until his third year. I had to endure two years of this? I couldn't imagine waiting that long to enjoy teaching.

There was a huge disconnect in my mind between how teaching was going and how things really *should* be going. The principal, other teachers, and some of the students told me I was doing a great job, but I could only think about the things that weren't going as well as I wanted them to.

After just a couple of weeks of teaching, it started getting so bad that Gary and I decided I should go to the doctor.

I was finally ready to admit there was a problem.

SEEING THE DOCTOR FOR HELP

I went off to school and Gary did some calling for me. I couldn't get in to see my regular doctor, but I could get in at another clinic. I made it to the end of the school day and then Gary drove me to the appointment. I held it together as the nurse took my vitals. I even managed some small talk as we figured out that her daughter was in one of my Spanish classes.

When she asked why I was there that day I started to come undone. Tears flowed as I explained my symptoms. Gary added his observations and then the nurse left the room while we waited for the doctor.

Now I was even more anxious. I didn't want one of my students to know that I was feeling so bad. (Later in the appointment the nurse promised she wouldn't say anything to her daughter.)

When the doctor came in, we talked about my symptoms. He left for a few minutes, conferred with a local psychiatrist, and came back with some recommended medicines for the anxiety and depression.

The doctor must have realized that the idea of taking something upset me. He told me that people go through similar feelings in a variety of jobs. "If you knew how many people come to see me and have to take medications for depression and anxiety . . .," he reassured.

That didn't really make me feel much better. Knowing that bank presidents and nurses and insurance agents and people in all sorts of professions were also struggling with depression and anxiety kind of scared me. I wanted the assurance that most people have it all together, not that we're all falling apart.

The doctor prescribed an antidepressant for the depression (to be taken daily) and another medicine for the anxiety (as needed, in my case). I began taking the medication for depression right away. I usually took one of the anxiety pills at school before my first class started. It didn't really make me feel completely better, but I guess it did enough because I never did break down and cry in front of my classes.

I had finally admitted there was a problem and now I had some medicine as a possible solution.

In your own situation, can you see how the problem escalates when you don't admit there is a problem? If you're in the middle of a difficult situation right now, don't wait.

THE PERFECT STORM

As I said before, a teaching job may not seem like a very stressful situation to most people, but for me it was the last straw. A tendency toward depression ran in my family and I had experienced its ups and downs to varying degrees ever since college. Self-doubt, perfectionism, and people-pleasing had plagued me for years, but I was usually able to continue to function when I really wanted to accomplish something. This job was the perfect storm that stopped me dead in my tracks. Teaching pushed me into a downward spiral that quickly became clinical depression.

Ignoring the warning signs (more about this in Chapter 6) is a surefire way to find yourself extremely sick, hardly knowing how you got there. You must admit there is a problem before you can take the necessary steps to get away from the edge.

As you read this book, I hope you'll garner an arsenal of tools that can help you get back to a healthy place (and do it again and again as needed). There is help, but it's up to you to notice your feelings and symptoms and reach out to someone when you're starting to go toward the edge.

What about the person who won't admit there is a problem, but everyone in their life can see it? Maybe you're a loved one reading this book and your heart is aching because your spouse, child, or friend is struggling daily with the symptoms of anxiety, depression, or some other mental illness. Is there any hope for keeping that person away from the edge?

Of course there is! *As long as a person is alive, there is always hope.*

FIGHTING THROUGH FIVE STAGES

It can be hard to admit you have a problem. In some ways, it may be like going through what's commonly known as the five stages of grief:

- Denial. *I don't have a problem.* You may continue to plow through your days in denial of your symptoms even though you are nearing the edge. When a friend or family member tries to point it out, you may vehemently refute the possibility that anything is wrong. In the beginning, this may be something you do unconsciously, not willing to admit that all the signs and symptoms point toward a bout with a mental illness. You may try to work harder and point out how well you are functioning to prove you aren't depressed.

- Anger. *How dare you say I'm depressed!* You are likely to put an even bigger mask on and "buck up" so you don't show as many symptoms in front of your loved ones. Even though you may be feeling unhappy, you show anger when confronted. This often can take the form of isolation. You blame others for your problems.

- Bargaining. *Just give me a little more time, I'll do better.* It's the lie you tell yourself. You may see that you're slipping in certain areas, but you still don't want to admit you have a concern. You'll continue to flounder, getting worse and worse until you slide even further into the next stage.

- Depression. *Leave me alone. I just don't feel well.* This may seem strange because it's what you've been dealing with all along, but it may become even worse at this point—when all your efforts to deny, defuse with anger, and bargain are futile. You may give up trying to juggle those things and sink deeper into the mental illness. Loved ones may see your symptoms get more pronounced and have to get more forceful about getting you the help you need.

- Acceptance. *Okay, you're right. I am depressed.* You'll finally go to the hospital, take the medicine, see the counselor, or do whatever seems necessary to get to better mental health, but sometimes this is a measured acceptance. You'll do one of those things . . . but not all. You'll negotiate a solution.

THE RIGHT KIND OF ACCEPTANCE

A person may bounce around in this list throughout the onset of a mental illness, but complete acceptance is the best way to move toward health and wholeness. Acceptance, however, needs to be positively focused. Negative acceptance could lead to just enduring the symptoms and not fighting to feel better. Instead, a person needs to admit they have a problem and do everything possible to get to a better emotional place.

There may be some frustrating times when you have measured success with treatments and decide to stop before you get to lasting stability—a place where your good mental health will last. You feel good so you decide you no longer need your medications. You're handling life better, so you cancel the appointment with your therapist. Make sure you're talking to your support system as you make decisions like that so your doctor or family member can point out if there's a need to continue or bring certain tools back into your recovery process.

WE ARE RESPONSIBLE FOR OUR OWN HEALTH

Ultimately, we are each in charge of our own emotional health. Each person must come to the point where they admit they have a problem and allow others to help them.

I can't be there for every single person I hear about who suffers from depression and anxiety. Taking on that burden could very well plunge me right back into depression myself. Instead, I need to trust that God will bring the right people into their lives so they know they're loved and worthy of getting help. We're all responsible for our own well-being. I can't expect my husband to boost my self-esteem. I can't expect him to coddle me when I'm feeling down. I can enjoy his love, encouragement, and care when he's feeling like showing those things to me, but I can't fall apart when he's going through his own stressful time and neglects to show those characteristics to me at the level I desire. I must keep checking my own thoughts and feelings and make sure I'm staying healthy.

In my case, I had finally admitted there was a problem and gone to the doctor. I started taking medications, but that wasn't enough to keep me from going over the edge.

Staying Away from the Edge Takeaways

- ⚜ We have to admit there is a problem if we want to get better.

- ⚜ Ignoring the warning signs can send us into a downward spiral of depression.

- ⚜ We may go through denial, anger, bargaining, and more depression, but we need to come to a place of acceptance so we can get the help we need.

- ⚜ Ultimately, we're each responsible for our own well-being.

Chapter 3

Medicine Takes Time

A cheerful heart is good medicine, but a crushed spirit dries up the bones. (Proverbs 17:22 NIV)

Medications for depression can take a few weeks to start being effective and even longer to reach their full level of efficiency. I had finally admitted there was a problem and been prescribed an antidepressant. I attempted to hang in there and wait for it to take effect, but my symptoms continued to worsen, and my negative thoughts probably canceled out any good the medicine could possibly do for me.

SOMETIMES YOU NEED MORE THAN JUST POSITIVE THINKING

Initially, I tried hard to keep a good attitude. Every day on the way to school I would play a CD by Jenny Simmons called *Becoming*. My son Dylan (a freshman at the time) probably knew something was wrong because he rode with me almost every day and I would usually cry as I listened to the CD. If he happened to ride the bus instead, I would really belt out the songs. Crying as I sang, I tried to believe that this was all going to work out for the best. If I could hang in there, things would get better, and I would love being a teacher. It was who I was "becoming," and it was going to be awesome. The first couple of songs on the CD were so good. I thought I could feel better if I really listened to them and believed their words. I especially loved to listen to the song *What Faith's About* and dream that I could be going into the best days of my whole life if I could just keep trying.[1]

I guess you can't just sing yourself out of a clinical depression, although focusing on uplifting, hopeful songs could be beneficial as part of the treatment for a mental illness.

***

MAYBE IF I JUST RELAX IT WILL GET BETTER

As the semester went on, it got more overwhelming because some students fell behind in their homework and I wasn't well enough to keep on top of it. I was barely keeping my head above water and the technology

---

1   Jenny Simmons, "What Faith's About" (https://www.youtube.com/watch?v=nxIfNz5biUw).

problems just sent waves of despair that threatened to drown me.

My flailing brain sometimes stumbled across this possibly helpful thought: "I just need to relax!" I wanted to ask the other teachers how they did that (but I never did). I wanted to know how they could come to school every day and not be anxious about what might happen in their classrooms. I had moments where I enjoyed what we were doing, but more often I was analyzing every comment and facial expression and trying to do things perfectly.

¿PERFECTO? ¡NO!

In those beginning days of teaching, I made a big deal in class about not trying to be perfect. I explained (in Spanish) that the students were going to make mistakes as they learned to speak. That was okay, I assured them. It was all part of the learning process. In each class, I pointed to every person in the room, one at a time, and asked the class a simple question: ¿Justin es perfecto? ¿Abbie es perfecta? ¿La Señora M es perfecta? Each time, the class answered correctly: No. I wrote the word *Perfecto* on the board, drew a huge circle around it, then crossed it out with my red marker. "¿Perfecto? ¡No!" As I looked around, I could see that they got it. They didn't have to be perfect. They could relax, have fun, and do their best as they learned Spanish.

Unfortunately, I couldn't follow my own advice. I was the teacher. I didn't want to make mistakes or admit that I didn't know how to do something. If a student asked me how to say a word and I didn't know, I just laughed and said I'd have to look it up, but inside it really bothered me that I didn't know. I felt embarrassed, and the heavy weight of trying to be perfect quickly altered my brain chemistry and a deep depression was the ultimate result. "Perfecto—No" was not the motto by which I was living.

THE LAST STRAW

I was usually a very kind, compassionate teacher, but I did get angry the last day I taught. I probably didn't let it show on the outside, but it boiled up on the inside.

Some of the students wouldn't quit messing around and I got even more frustrated than usual. We also had a tornado alarm that day and one class had to go hang out in the girls' bathroom for a few minutes. When we got back to the room, I was perplexed to find that my dry erase markers had disappeared. I looked all over and couldn't find them. The students seemed innocent. If someone knew what had happened, they did a good job hiding it. I think I managed to find another stash of markers up in one of my cupboards so we could keep doing our review game, but it was maddening.

Additionally, one of the students in Spanish 4 was frustrated with me during a test that day because she felt like we hadn't covered some of the things being asked. I tried to reassure her that it would be okay, but she was very upset as we ended class. I was too.

I didn't want to disappoint and frustrate my students, but it was happening more and more often. At first, they were patient when I couldn't get them into the online quiz or the digital textbook. When it kept happening, they understandably got annoyed.

I didn't have the skills needed to counter the ongoing problems, and the medicine just couldn't work fast enough to keep me from spiraling down.

WAITING IS SO HARD

I know waiting for medications to take effect can be a problem for many who suffer from depression or another mental illness. If they could remove themselves from the difficult situation and just rest until the medicine provided its full benefit, they might be fine, but most people don't have that luxury. They have to keep going to the stressful job or living with the difficult person or looking at the empty chair at the table. Often, they continue getting closer and closer to the edge despite the medication working to correct their faulty brain chemistry.

Medications can be a difficult part of living with a mental illness. Psychiatrists or family physicians can prescribe an antidepressant or other medication for the depression or anxiety a person may be experiencing, but it is not an exact science. People react in different ways to each medication. What works well for one person can produce side effects that are unacceptable for someone else. The person with the sickness must wait for several weeks to see if the medication prescribed is effective. If the side effects are bothersome and they decide, with their doctor, to try something else, then they usually need to taper off the first drug before they give the second medicine a try. Naturally, a person can get discouraged and frustrated when they are going through this waiting process. That's part of the reason I had to go to the hospital. The medicine wasn't working, and I was thinking very negatively. My hope was gone and I had to get help before I did something irreversible.

TO MEDICATE OR NOT TO MEDICATE?

Once you get on a medication for mental illness, will you need to stay on it for the rest of your life? Possibly. Or maybe not.

Every person's situation is different, so we're not able to make sweeping generalizations when it comes to medicines. Some people may need to take something indefinitely, but others may be able to go off their prescription once they've done some counseling and reached a more stable emotional place.

When someone finds a medicine that works well for them, it can be surprising and discouraging to find that it sometimes stops working later and they must consult with their doctor to find a different medication or a different dosage to combat their illness.

Women who are pregnant have the difficult decision about whether or not they should take medicines, considering the risk of harm to their unborn baby. Back in 1999, when we lived in Iowa, I was struggling with strong feelings of anger and despair. I even got a prescription for an antidepressant, but I didn't take it because I was pregnant. I think that was the right decision for me at the time, but I know I had to endure a lot of very uncomfortable feelings because I chose to not take medicine to help offset those emotions.

People have strong opinions about medications. *You* may have a strong opinion. *I'm* never *going to take a medication!* or *I will* never *be able to go off my medicine!*

Let's look at those extremes.

THE ABSOLUTELY-NO-MEDICINE CAMP

If you do an internet search for "no medication for anxiety and depression," you'll find over one hundred million results. That's an overwhelming amount of info to sort through as you consider if it's right for you to avoid taking a pill for your mental illness.

Many of those results may take you to sites that present scientific evidence that there are alternative treatments for depression and anxiety, but the vast majority of the results will show someone's strongly worded opinion that you should *never* rely on pharmaceuticals when you have a mental illness. This often adds guilt to the decision-making process.

THE MEDICINE-FOREVER CAMP

Typing "taking medicine for depression and anxiety indefinitely" into the search bar brings up over twenty-four million results. Even though it's less than the "no-medicine" search, it's still going to take you a long time to peruse the opinions about never going off your depression or anxiety medicine.

Once you get on a medication, it can be frightening to consider living without it, especially if you experience bothersome symptoms when you forget to take it for a couple of days. If mental illness runs in your family, your doctor may urge you to consider staying on a medicine for the rest of your life.

All these differing recommendations can be daunting. It's best to not limit yourself to one camp or the other, but to move forward slowly as you make your decisions.

IS MEDICINE REALLY NECESSARY?

So, you've started taking a medication for your depression or anxiety. It helps, but you aren't sure you want to take it forever. Are you stuck taking it indefinitely just because you were diagnosed with a mental illness?

It's such a tricky thing because people will argue, "Well, you wouldn't expect a diabetic to go off their medication, would you?" No, of course not. Acute diabetics aren't able to get off their insulin. But with a better diet and a good exercise program, some people who are *borderline* diabetic can reduce medications and avoid having to go on insulin. It just depends on if the disease has advanced.

The same thing applies to depression and other mental illnesses. People who deal with anxiety or minor depression can learn skills and habits that will help them deal with their symptoms. They may be able to learn to think in ways that *could* allow them to reduce or remove their medicine.

However, you should *always* consult with your doctor before going off any medication—whether it's for a physical illness or a mental illness. They need to monitor you as you make the change to something different or completely go off a medication. Your loved ones should also be involved in the decision to change or discontinue a medicine. They can observe you and your behavior, as well as provide support as you transition to either a different medicine or to life without it.

So, medications can help someone who experiences the symptoms of a mental illness. But medicines might not be enough to get everyone back to a stable mindset. We also need to consider counseling so we can learn better ways of thinking—something that can get us out of a continued downward spiral.

Without that extra help, some of us may even find ourselves in the basement, picking up an extension cord as we contemplate whether we want life or death.

Staying Away from the Edge Takeaways

- ℞ Medications can take a few weeks to start being effective.

- ℞ ¿Perfecto? ¡No! Perfectionism can be a major contributor to mental illness.

- ℞ Be patient as you wait to see if your medicine works. (And be even more patient if you have to try something else!)

- ℞ *Always* consult your doctor before changing the dosage or going off your medication.

Chapter 4

Choose Life or Death

This day I call the heavens and the earth as witnesses against you that I have set before you life and death, blessings and curses. Now choose life, so that you and your children may live. (Deuteronomy 30:19 NIV)

After I threw the extension cord to the ground, I trudged up the basement stairs and sat down to attempt some more work on my lesson plans. I couldn't concentrate. I didn't know what I should do in each class. Minutes and then hours went by and I still had just as many blank spaces in my planner. Grades were due on Monday, and I didn't even know how I was going to turn those in on time.

My husband came in from his day of work as a pastor and saw me sitting in tears at our kitchen table. "How's it going?" he asked innocently. I let it all out then, crying.

"Shhh," he urged. He led me over to the den where we could talk without scaring our two teenage sons.

I could hardly get the words out as I tried to express all my emotions to Gary. "I can't do this! I don't even want to! I don't know what I'm doing! It's just not worth it! I can't do it!" Then I admitted that I had gone to the basement and wrapped the extension cord around my neck. "I wasn't going to do anything, but it really scared me, you know?"

Hearing that scared him too.

"Robyn, I think it's time for us to get you some help. Do you need to go right now?"

Choking back sobs, I told him I felt like I had to get my grades figured out first. That's me, always the responsible one. I wanted to die, but first I had to turn in my midterm grades.

We talked some more, and I assured him I wouldn't do anything to harm myself. We decided we would go to the hospital the next day. I sat back down, added up grades, and entered them in my online gradebook, all the while brushing away tears. My heart hurt more when I saw that some students were missing grades on several assignments. I hadn't been well enough to get those taken care of in a timely manner. I finally finished what I could and went to bed, but I worried about the decision to go to the hospital. Did I really have to go?

On the one hand, I looked forward to getting the help I needed. On the other, I feared what a step like this would do to my reputation. What would people think? Sleep was a long time in coming. I woke up again with a continued mixture of hope and dread. As hopeless as everything seemed, though, I was choosing life.

STATISTICS ARE FRIGHTENING, BUT WE HAVE A CHOICE

Worldwide, more than 700,000 people die each year from suicide. We are saddened by news of the untimely deaths of celebrities we know and love, but it is devastating when a friend or family member dies this way.

According to the World Health Organization (WHO), for every suicide there are many more people who attempt to do so.[1]

I'm praying you'll realize it all comes down to a choice. Yes, our brain chemistry may get messed up at some point, making it more likely that we may do something out of character, but I truly believe we can— *we must*—make a choice to live. Hopefully we'll do that before we get too close to that dangerous edge.

If we decide that death by suicide is not an option, it is imperative that we reach out for help when we realize

---

1   https://www.who.int/news-room/fact-sheets/detail/suicide

we're starting to drown in our negative thoughts, despair, and hopelessness. Everything in us will scream that death would be better, but we can't believe that lie. Sure, our temporary problems and frustrations will be over for us, but we will leave behind so many people who will wonder what they could have done to keep us here on this earth. The hurt never ends—it's just transferred to those we leave behind.

MOST PEOPLE WILL GRIEVE THE LOSS

There may be people who won't care. You hear about them every once in a while on the news. The cruel teenage girl that urged her boyfriend to die by suicide and suggested ways for him to do it.[2] The bullies in a school who teased and taunted a classmate so much that the student finally decided to end their own life.[3] The trolls on social media who hid behind their anonymity and bullied someone who spoke up against cyberbullying until she eventually died by suicide.[4] These are the widely publicized exceptions to the rule.

The vast majority of people will be heartbroken when they find out someone has died by suicide. They

---

2   https://en.wikipedia.org/wiki/Manslaughter_of_Conrad_Roy

3   https://www.nytimes.com/2010/03/30/us/30bully.html

4   https://www.abc.net.au/news/2014-02-23/charlotte-dawson-death-puts-focus-on-cyber-bullying/5277904?nw=0

will mourn the loss of life, whether they knew that person closely or not.

Each person is special, and God has a plan for their life. A loss to something like suicide leaves behind a gaping hole that will never be filled. We need to decide to keep living, even though it will be painful at times.

WHAT DECIDING TO LIVE MEANS

Deciding to live might mean you need to spend some time in a hospital setting. It could also lead you to recover at home, taking a break from the pressures of life.

I ended up in the hospital. I hadn't gone to the most extreme measures, but my hopelessness and the episode with the extension cord were enough to warrant that level of care. If you're feeling hopeless, it's vital that you choose life and get help instead of carrying out the thoughts in your mind that would lead to death. I'll talk more about what it was like to be admitted to the hospital later in this book. I wish I could say that all my suicidal thoughts ended after I got help, but that hasn't been the case.

For me, the opportunity to choose life over death comes quite regularly. For some strange reason, my brain seems to default to thoughts of ending it all when I get extremely stressed, tired, or overwhelmed.

I entertained those intrusive thoughts way too often in the years leading up to my depressive episode in 2014. Of course, we can't think ourselves out of clinical depression, but there may be a point early on where catching those suicidal ideations is possible. I've been working with a counselor recently, hoping to get to the root of those thoughts and get rid of them once and for all. I'm learning that I do have some control over what I'm thinking. If and when those thoughts come around, I want to catch them and change them to more positive thoughts as quickly as possible.

FIGHTING SUICIDAL THOUGHTS

Is it a sin to think those thoughts? No, but it could turn into sin if we choose to keep thinking them. We can't control every random thought that pops into our heads, but we can control where our minds dwell.

Can I do anything to change those negative thoughts? I'm working on that. I've come to realize that it's comparable to feeling an urge to do other things that wouldn't be good for me: the urge to eat when I'm not hungry; the urge to check Facebook or my email because I'm stressed and don't want to work on something difficult or stressful; the urge to lash out when I'm upset.

We don't have to give in when we feel an urge. Just like someone can't *make* me do anything I don't want to do unless they have authority over me, I don't *have* to go with whatever thoughts try to crowd into my brain. I can make the *choice* to think about something else, just like I can (but often don't) choose to do something else instead of overeating, scrolling mindlessly through Facebook, or lashing out in anger or frustration.

So much of what we think, feel, and do in life comes down to the choices we make. Our brain will want to revert to whatever it normally thinks, but we can choose to think better thoughts and get to a healthier emotional place. This in turn often brings us to a better physical or spiritual frame of mind, and vice versa.

DO YOU WANT TO BE WELL?

The Bible tells a story about the paralytic by the pool of Bethesda in John 5. Jesus asks the man, "Do you want to be well?" At first, the lame man gives some excuse about not being able to get in the pool when the waters are stirring, but eventually he has to tell Jesus, "Yes, I want to get well." Without the man's commitment to his own healing, Jesus isn't going to grant him what he needs.

Is that all that's necessary for those of us with a mental health diagnosis? Do we just need to name it and claim it? Not necessarily. I'm sure many would say, "Yes, I want to be well," but they continue to struggle with how they're feeling. Still—commiting to our own recovery seems essential.

IT ALL COMES DOWN TO A CHOICE

Even if someone can't be completely healed, I think it still comes down to a choice. A choice to keep going in spite of the pain. A choice to try to see glimmers of hope in the darkness. A choice to connect with people even though they sometimes hurt you (on purpose or accidentally). A choice to be a part of this big wide world even though it all seems purposeless at times. Or—when we're really struggling—a choice to share our dark thoughts with someone and let them protect us from ourselves.

It's such a hard thing to deal with, because sometimes we *can* make the choice to think better, to get out of bed even though we don't really feel like it, to focus on the positive things in our lives, and to enjoy living. Other days we really can be too sick to take those actions.

What is the answer? Do what we can when we can. Show ourselves grace on the days when we "can't." Never give up, no matter how we're feeling. That's the only way we'll avoid going over the edge.

The truth is, it's up to each and every person to choose life. And *keep* choosing it when the junk that life throws at you pushes you up to the figurative edge. Keep choosing it when you're staring down in terror, afraid you won't be able to keep yourself from plummeting over. Keep choosing life when you're afraid you're going to actually throw yourself over, not caring what happens once you begin your fall. Keep choosing life when you feel the uncontrollable slide and you feel the edge approaching.

I hope you'll see that making the decision to live will eventually lead to a life where you can thrive most of the time—not just white-knuckle it and endure. We'll explore several ways to get to a place of thriving in Part 3. Right now, you just need to recognize that you have a choice between life and death.

You can choose to live and come back from the edge.

Staying Away from the Edge Takeaways

   🎵 As hopeless as life sometimes seems, we need to choose life.

   🎵 Once we decide suicide is not an option, we need to reach out for help.

   🎵 Each person is special and God has a plan for their life.

   🎵 It's not a sin to have suicidal thoughts, but it could become sin if we choose to keep thinking them.

   🎵 Do you want to be well? (We have to answer yes and realize we have some work ahead of us.)

   🎵 Do what you can when you can (and show yourself grace when you can't).

   🎵 Keep choosing life.

Chapter 5

Coming Back from the Edge

So do not fear, for I am with you; do not be dismayed, for I am your God. I will strengthen you and help you; I will uphold you with my righteous right hand. (Isaiah 41:10 NIV)

My hopelessness landed me in the hospital. Once I got there, there really was no place to go but up (assuming that I now was choosing life). While they tweaked my medications, I attended group sessions to learn how to come back from the dark place I was in.

I soaked up every topic sheet they passed out to us. I had heard some of it before: taking medications, catastrophization (expecting the worst possible outcome for a situation), and ruminating (excessive thinking about a problem). Other concepts were new: having a plan to stay healthy, getting off the merry-go-round of guilt, coping with anxiety, and having a support system. Exploring every topic in a group setting with the guidance of a counselor was helpful, even though

I wasn't always thinking clearly enough to apply every tool they presented.

I spent nearly a week in the hospital, resting and learning. While others were anxious to get back to their children and families, I was content to stay there. I wasn't ready to go back quite so soon.

I'M NOT SUPPOSED TO BE HERE!

In a group session one day, the counselor mentioned that the hospital was really for acute cases. I looked around the table at my fellow patients. One woman was dozing fitfully from the meds they had her on. Another guy rocked back and forth in his chair, seemingly unable to focus on what our leader was saying. A couple of women looked interested and alert, even though they had just arrived the day before. It hit me like a ton of bricks, and I suddenly realized that I shouldn't be there. I was taking up a spot that was needed for someone who was much sicker than I was.

After the session, I went to the nurses' station. I tearfully apologized and said that I shouldn't be there. I repeated what the counselor had said about the hospital being for acute cases, but the nurse assured me that it was fine that I was still there. It was too late in the day to really do anything to have me released. I had to wait and talk to the doctor the next morning. When I talked to Gary on the phone later, he said that he had thought I was going to ask about going home earlier in the day and then I felt even worse.

All those feelings of shame and self-loathing were part of my problem, even though at the time I thought *I'm well! I don't need to be here!*

The next day I got to talk to the doctor and went through the process of getting released. Gary picked me up and I said a few goodbyes to the other patients on my way out. I was finally ready to leave. Of course, I was not completely well, but I was on my way back from the edge.

THINGS LOOKED DIFFERENT

On the way home, I saw everything through new eyes. The sky was more blue. It felt like the sun shone just for me. It was such a contrast from the previously dark, dreary landscape brought on by my despair.

I had quit the teaching job, so I didn't have any pressure to put on a happy face and get back to work. I was able to rest, go to counseling, and figure out what I could do so I didn't have to go back to the hospital again.

HOPE FINALLY RETURNS

I didn't have very much fear the day I came home. I was weary, but I had hope. Hope that life would get better.

Hope that I wouldn't ever get that sick again. I think I was even starting to think about the hope I could give to others who were feeling the same way.

When I went to the doctor the week after I came home from the hospital, the nurse at the clinic gave me a big hug. Then my doctor did the same thing when she came in. I was so touched that they cared enough to do that. It would have been easy to stay professional and just deal with the appointment without that personal touch. It felt good to be loved like that.

I went to church and felt the love of people there too. With no options to explain my absence the previous Sunday morning, Gary had shared from the pulpit that I had been hospitalized for depression. It was a difficult morning for him, but it allowed our church family to be part of the healing process.

So many people cared and made sure they told me. While I was in the hospital, I got cards from church members and pictures created by kids in our student ministry programs. Many people don't have that level of support, or they suffer in silence because they're afraid to tell anyone, due to the stigma that still surrounds mental health issues.

✳ ✳ ✳

GETTING BACK TO NORMAL

So, you've experienced a mental health crisis. Maybe you spent some time in a hospital or you had an intense time of crisis at home. Wherever you were, hopefully you made the decision to choose life, and now you face the long climb out of your pit of despair. How do you get back to "normal" life again?

Hopefully you have the support of your family, but you may need to be proactive about surrounding yourself with help as you come back from the edge. Your counselor or doctor is a major part of that support system. If you are part of a church family, you could talk to individuals there about being a source of assistance for you. Attending a support group like Fresh Hope can really help (more about that in Chapter 13). You can search for online social media groups that can provide a safe place for you to vent about how you're feeling, ask questions about your illness, and receive encouraging words from people who understand what you're going through.

A HIKING ANALOGY

Gary and I love to go hiking. We've been to the Grand Canyon several times and have hiked all the way to the bottom. The first time we visited, we drove to the park the evening before we hiked. We walked along the edge, looking out over this beautiful, impressive landscape.

We drove to the west end of the canyon and watched the shadows change as the sun set. My dad was with us, and all three of us had nightmares that night about hiking the next day.

We saw the depth of the canyon (and we couldn't even see all the way to the bottom!) and we had a healthy fear of what could happen. We had all heard stories about someone who had either camped too close to the edge and fallen over, slipped while they were on one of the trails and plunged to their death, or had misjudged where they were stepping as they took a selfie and fell.

Even though many people have died at the Grand Canyon, there are thousands of people that hike its trails each year. Why? Because of the beauty. Because of the thrill of seeing the landscape and the harsh conditions along the trails to and from the bottom. They hike because they want to challenge themselves and feel a sense of pride when they emerge from the deep canyon after climbing for hours.

The key is having a great respect for the edge of the Grand Canyon. You can't just traipse along, not paying attention to where your feet are going and where the edge of the trail is. That's a sure way to go over, with no hope of coming back out alive.

But if you approach the edge with caution, stopping well back from that dangerous line, planting your feet and being aware of your surroundings, then you can look out over that great expanse and enjoy its magnificent beauty. You can even descend below the rim of the canyon, sticking to the trail and making sure people know where you are so that they can come find you if you get in trouble.

THE JOURNEY OF MENTAL ILLNESS

Living with a mental illness is similar to navigating the Grand Canyon. A person can't just rush through life at a breakneck speed, ignoring the figurative edge and the danger signs as they're getting emotionally close. They need to be familiar with the edge and the warning signs. If they have some down days, they don't have to throw themselves over that edge. They can stick to life's trail, relying on others to travel down the path with them and help them get back out when the time is right.

There's even beauty in the down times of living with a mental illness. Going through hard times can remind us of what other people are going through. Sometimes we can learn more about ourselves during our "over the edge" times and it will make us even stronger and healthier when we're back at the top. Art, music, and writing that people have created during their dark times can be comforting and inspirational for others who sometimes struggle with similar feelings.

Am I trying to imply that we should go careening over the edge since it can result in good things? For heaven's sake, no! I assume you picked up a copy of this book because you have gone over that emotional edge at some point (or gotten dangerously close). Thankfully, it didn't result in death. Since you're still here, you are blessed with the opportunity to get to a better place emotionally. You don't have to live down in the depths of despair you felt during your initial crisis. You've gotten help—either through medication, counseling, or both—and now you can, hopefully, live a life that is aware of the edge. A life that respects the edge and carefully maneuvers away from that dangerous place when the stresses and strains of life apply their pressure.

A person would be a fool if they unrolled their sleeping bag on the very edge of the Grand Canyon, climbed in, and promptly fell asleep. That person is just asking for a very rude awakening—if they wake up at all. Instead, a smart camper will find a safe place far back from the edge of the canyon and set up camp there. They can walk over and enjoy the view, but they must respect the danger of the drop-off in front of them.

A person with a high risk for mental illness must be careful as they go through life. They need to be aware of how their brain responds to different stressors. When they experience a loss or something traumatic, they need to be deliberate about their self-care so they don't find themselves over the edge with no way to get back out by themselves.

Let's agree that the edge is not an unmanageable place to be, but our behavior on that edge is what can be risky. Are we reckless and impulsive? That's irresponsible and dangerous. Are we purposeful and careful? That's beneficial and helpful.

I spent almost a week in the hospital before I felt well enough to go home and face my life. Even though I felt better, I knew that I had a lifetime of learning to deal with depression so I didn't end up back in the hospital.

Let's back up now and look at how we even get to the edge in the first place.

Staying Away from the Edge Takeaways

- 🦇 Surround yourself with help after a mental health crisis.

- 🦇 Like the Grand Canyon, you need to respect the edge in order to stay safe.

- 🦇 It's possible to find beauty in the down times of life.

- 🦇 Since you've made it back from "over the edge," you have the opportunity to get to a healthier place emotionally.

- 🦇 Being deliberate about self-care will help keep you away from the edge.

Part 2: Approaching the Edge

Chapter 6

Brushes with the Edge

The prudent see danger and take refuge,
but the simple keep going and pay the penalty.
(Proverbs 27:12 NIV)

Staring at my tear-streaked face in the mirror, I hated what I saw. The lines around my mouth were turned down in a hard frown. My eyes looked wild and red. I turned away and sat on the edge of the bathtub and tried to collect my thoughts. Taking care of three kids while my husband was attending college classes was hard! How would I handle it once the next baby arrived? I put my hands on my extended belly and started crying again. I wanted to be the cheerful, relaxed mom who loved spending time with her children, but it seemed like I was losing it on a regular basis lately. A squabble between at least two of my kids in the next room finally registered on my radar. I swiped a hand over my face to get rid of the tears, took a deep breath, and opened the door to face my brood.

***

GETTING TOO CLOSE TO THE EDGE

In my younger years, I often skirted the edge. Sometimes I stayed on solid ground and accomplished the things expected of me. I did well in school and was a very responsible person. I hated to disappoint anyone, so I did my best to do my best. If I did mess up and disappoint my parents, a friend, or myself, there would be tears and a long mourning period before I finally let something go and moved on with life.

Looking back, I can see many times in my life when I got dangerously close to the edge. I probably had one foot extended over the abyss and only the grace of God kept me from plummeting over.

I was a pretty happy kid. Friends in middle school commented about the smile that was usually on my face and the way I bounced as I walked. I loved Jesus and I wanted to share his love with others, even though I was too shy to be very vocal about my faith. I started taking Spanish in high school and began to dream about being a missionary in some Spanish-speaking country after college. I had some bouts with negative emotions, but I normally bounced back to my happy demeanor quickly.

When I got to college, my emotional health got quite a bit more unstable. I was on my own for the first time in my life, attending a Christian college about seven hundred miles from home. It was challenging to get used to college homework and establish new friendships. When I socialized a little too much, my grades dropped, and I was in danger of losing my scholarship. It wasn't a huge part of my financial aid package, but I can remember feeling so much anxiety and shame when that first semester's grade report came out.

I started to get more stressed as pressures mounted. Add to that the stereotypical college schedule (late nights studying and/or hanging out with friends) and I experienced mood swings. Sometimes I would be excited about the fun I was having with my friends and other times I would feel depressed that I wasn't getting my work done.

I hardly understood what was happening to me as I rode the roller coaster of emotions from day to day. Once I had a French horn lesson with my band director and my mood was quite flat. I hardly talked to him, and I didn't act very interested in what we were practicing. He remarked that I was very *lethargic* that day. I didn't know what that meant, but I really didn't care.

EVEN LOVE COULDN'T FIX IT

During my senior year, I met Gary. At that time, he was a farmer. There were lots of ups and downs during our dating years as I struggled with idealism, perfectionism, and pessimism. I tried to break up with Gary three times. I loved him, but I thought maybe I was supposed to be a missionary and not get married. Looking back, I can see that my thinking was quite distorted during this time, and it led to more anxiety and bouts with mild depression. After lots of prayers and conversations, I finally felt peace and we got engaged.

This city girl had to adjust to life on an Iowa farm after we got married. I loved seeing the baby pigs and helping in the hog house, but it seemed like every time I learned to do something new on the farm, I cried. Watching corn unload into the bin, riding beans (we rode on a seat in front of a tractor and sprayed any weeds we saw in the rows below us), learning to do fall tillage, and almost any other chore brought tears because I was so nervous that I was going to do something wrong. My poor husband probably wondered if I would ever enjoy being a farm wife.

MAYBE BECOMING A PARENT WILL HELP

We had our first daughter, Erin, in October of 1992. I cried almost the entire forty-five-minute drive home from the hospital because I was so nervous about being a new mom. *What if I mess this child up?*

A few months after our second child, Allison, was born in June of 1994, I went through about a year of anger toward my children. I felt terribly guilty whenever I would lash out at them, but I couldn't seem to control it. I read everything I could get my hands on and asked my Bible study group to pray for me, but I continued to struggle. Most of the anger suddenly disappeared after about a year. Looking back, I think I may have been suffering from postpartum depression, but it was never diagnosed.

Blake was born in May of 1997. It was fun to add a little boy to our growing family and we enjoyed a couple of good years on the farm. I can't remember how much I dealt with depression during those years, but I know I experienced the ups and downs all moms go through when they're taking care of young children.

After Gary felt his call into ministry (that could probably be another book—but he'll have to write that one!), we moved into a rental house in Orange City so Gary could attend college. I was pregnant, and that's when I considered taking an antidepressant but decided against it. Dylan was born in March of 2000, completing our family of six.

ANOTHER MOVE BRINGS MORE DEPRESSION

After two years of college for Gary, I went through another time of depression during our move from Iowa to Michigan so he could go to seminary. That time it got so intense that I ended up going on medication and talking to a counselor for a few months. I stayed on the medication for several years and then gradually weaned myself off it and stayed relatively stable until the teaching job came along. There were days when I felt down and discouraged, but it usually passed within a short amount of time.

As the years went by, I still had times where I had bad days and struggled with feeling weepy or anxious, but it usually didn't affect my daily routine and I never felt like I had to go back on medication. I had told myself that I would do that if my depression got bad again, but secretly I saw that as a weakness and hoped I could manage without medicines.

***

SYMPTOMS USUALLY PROGRESS

Very seldom does someone suddenly attempt suicide. There is usually a progression of symptoms over the years until the person finally goes over the edge.

So, what are those symptoms? Mental illness can manifest in many ways, often starting with some items on this list:

Loss of interest in things you normally enjoy (hobbies, sports, time with friends, sex)

Sleep problems (either sleeping way too much or not being able to sleep)

Changes in eating (overeating or loss of appetite)

Unexplained aches and pains (headaches, back trouble, other physical problems)

Loss of focus (trouble concentrating, thinking, remembering, making decisions)

Depressed mood (feelings of sadness, emptiness, hopelessness, crying, mood swings)

Irritation (feelings of anger, irritability, or frustration—especially common in men)

Anxiety (agitation or restlessness)

Lethargy (slowed speaking, thinking, or movements)

Death (thinking about it often, wishing for it, suicidal thoughts and actions)

Everyone's illness is different. Not everyone will experience all these symptoms. If you notice several of them and they last for more than two weeks, it's time to get professional help.

Many people ignore the warning signs for depression and power through their low mood and lack of interest in life. Sometimes the depression lifts and they feel like themselves again. Depression will come and go, kind of like dealing with the annoying symptoms of a cold or the flu.

Others will suffer with a low-grade depression for years, not even realizing they're depressed. They get used to how they're feeling, and they don't even consider the possibility of feeling better.

How sad that so many people—knowingly or unknowingly—slog through life with so little enjoyment and so much physical and emotional pain.

The everyday challenges and frustrations of life can add to someone's depression, and eventually they may even be pushed over the edge by an inciting incident.

Staying Away from the Edge Takeaways

- 🎣 They say hindsight is 20/20. You may be able to see brushes with the edge as you look back at different seasons of your life.

- 🎣 Go over the list of symptoms in this chapter and think about times when you experienced several of them. Those were brushes with the edge.

- 🎣 For some people, depression comes and goes.

- 🎣 Others may experience a low-grade depression for years and never realize they're depressed.

Chapter 7

An Inciting Incident

*And we know that in all things God works for the good
of those who love him, who have been called according to his
purpose. (Romans 8:28 NIV)*

I've loved writing ever since elementary school. My
story structure in third grade needed some work, but I've
learned to recognize a good plot after years of reading
and writing. In writing a story, an inciting incident (or,
as someone once referred to it, an "exciting incident") is
an event that thrusts the protagonist into the main action
of the story.

As the main character in my own life story, I had
gone through almost forty-eight years of living with
just occasional brushes with the edge. It was intense
at times, and I felt strong emotions and fought against
hopelessness, but nothing had threatened to actually
push me over the edge until the teaching job. I had come
to my inciting incident.

Here's how it all happened back in 2014.

After subbing in our local school system for several years, a Spanish position opened up. I enjoyed getting to know the students and using my Spanish as I subbed, but I wasn't sure I wanted to teach full-time. But the longer I thought about it, the more excited I got. I talked it over with Gary and decided to apply. The interview went well, and they offered me the job. I was going to teach full-time again after a break of twenty-four years.

THIS IS GOING TO BE FUN!

The first couple of days of my new job were pretty easy—the students weren't there yet. I went through meetings with fellow teachers and spent time preparing my classroom for the school year. I was going to be the best Spanish teacher, I thought. I would teach so well that every student would love Spanish as much as I do.

Things didn't go according to plan.

As you saw in Part 1 of this book, the demands of my new job and my inability to deal with the emotions that bubbled up in me as I failed to live up to my own perfectionistic expectations soon brought me to a point of crisis.

My negative feelings about the job may have been a continuation of my tendency to flee difficult situations.

Early in our married life, I would often fantasize about what life would have been like if I hadn't gotten married and had moved to Spain to be a missionary instead. I only remembered the good times about my junior year in college when I lived with a family in Madrid and studied Spanish. When I was thinking more clearly, I could recall many frustrating situations while I studied abroad, but my depressed mind ignored those times and suggested that life would be better if I could just be in Spain instead. Fleeing mentally was a coping mechanism that may have contributed to later depressive episodes.

My inciting incident didn't lead to a great achievement and personal growth (at least not at that time). Instead, the teaching job pushed me right over the edge.

**

While many people deal with the annoying symptoms of a mental illness for years, there often is something more significant that takes a person into a time of serious illness, with symptoms that interfere with life.

POSSIBLE TRIGGERS

Here are some inciting incidents that *could* lead to mental illness, or even a complete breakdown:

- The death of a family member or close friend

- Changing jobs or schools

- Divorce

- Substance abuse

- Dysfunction in the family that gets worse until someone finally gets sick

- Rejection by a friend or family member

- A health-related diagnosis

Under the right circumstances, almost anything could become someone's inciting incident. The actual situation may be fairly common, and most people may be able to handle it, but for those with a predisposition for mental illness, that incident may be the impetus that leads to increased stress and anxiety. Eventually, it could even result in a full-blown crisis.

Staying Away from the Edge Takeaways

- 🕭 An inciting incident often contributes to someone going "over the edge."

- 🕭 If you are predisposed to mental illness, it's important to watch your mental health carefully when you go through stressful experiences.

Chapter 8

Stress and Anxiety Levels Rise

Why, my soul, are you downcast? Why so disturbed within me? Put your hope in God, for I will yet praise him, my Savior and my God. (Psalm 43:5 NIV)

As the days went by, I started to become more and more anxious and stressed. I got through my seven classes each day, but I couldn't really enjoy them because I was so worried about getting everything right. I couldn't concentrate on the students that liked Spanish. Instead, I worried about changing the minds of the students who frequently announced, "I hate Spanish." Statements like that don't help a teacher's confidence level. They didn't hate *me*, they were just frustrated with the new words they had to learn, but it was hard not to take it personally.

SYMPTOMS START PILING UP

Quite a few things were happening to me during the first couple of weeks of school. I was going to the bathroom more often. I lost my appetite and didn't eat much. Before this, I would usually clean my plate, but I found myself throwing away most of my lunch at school. By the time I went to the hospital I had lost about fifteen pounds. This was something I had been trying to do all summer, but my stress snacking had kept it from happening. My current situation was not a healthy way to lose weight.

I wasn't sleeping well at night, and I found it hard to relax when I wasn't at school. I would sit in front of my lesson plan book and stare at the white boxes I was expected to fill. I would sit and think "I can't do this!" instead of just deciding what to do in each class and getting my plans in place.

So much of the classroom routine had changed since I taught after college. Back then, I did everything on paper, but it had evolved into using mostly computers. I had to figure out how to give quizzes and tests online, keep track of grades on the computer, and use resources from the digital textbook to show grammar lessons and other things on the screen in the classroom. Sometimes they worked and sometimes they didn't.

When I tried to relax at night and watch a little television with Gary, my lesson plans were never far from my thoughts. My brows would knit together in a kind of permanent frown. When Gary would point that out, I tried to relax my face and smooth my eyebrows out, but soon they would go back to the worried wrinkle.

I started to lose control of student behavior in some of the classes. For some reason, it seemed to happen in the classes with fewer students. They would talk when they shouldn't and many of the kids were becoming disrespectful. They didn't like the new method and they wanted me to know it. I really liked all my students (well, most of the time), but it was frustrating to fight the growing chaos in a couple of classes.

EVEN GETTING HELP IS STRESSFUL

All of this was going on even after I had seen a doctor and started taking an antidepressant. The stress and anxiety continued to get worse until I finally lost hope and had my basement experience.

What I didn't expect was how stressful it would be to finally ask for help. I was an extremely sick woman the day my husband took me to the emergency room and I admitted that I was having thoughts about harming myself. They took my vitals, asked lots of questions, and had me change into blue scrubs as I waited for a social worker to find a place for me to go. As is often the case, their beds were full and they were looking into having me go to a facility that was farther away. I didn't want it to be an inconvenience for Gary to visit me. I tried to back out gracefully. "You know, I think I'll be okay at home." No, the nurse shook her head. Once a patient has expressed thoughts of self-harm the hospital needed to do whatever they could to keep the patient safe. I began to cry as I worried about where I might have to go.

A little later the nurse returned with good news. "A bed opened up at the hospital across town. We'll transport you by ambulance and your husband can meet you there." Once again, I tried to be helpful and not be a burden to anyone. "Gary can just drive me there," I offered.

She was kind but firm as she repeated herself. "No, once you've expressed thoughts of self-harm we are responsible for you. You need to go by ambulance." I swallowed my sobs and resigned myself to the fact that this was going to happen, even though I had changed my mind and really wanted to just go home.

I climbed up into the ambulance on my own and sat on a little seat behind the driver. It was so different from the time I rode in an ambulance after I broke my ankle. That time I was flat on my back, in pain, feeling every single bump in the road. This time I was able to ride in comfort, looking out the back window of the ambulance as we drove past familiar sights until we reached the hospital. The attendants riding with me couldn't see the emotional brokenness that was hurting me inside. Once we reached the other hospital, I was escorted into the emergency room area and placed in a room off to the side with just a couple of chairs. Gary joined me as soon as he got there.

After a while, a doctor came, asked more questions, and finished the admission process. I followed an orderly through a series of hallways to my temporary home away from home. Gary was at my side, holding my hand reassuringly. Our escort talked to someone through an intercom and the first door opened, then we waited while a second door was unlocked and I was led to the nurses' station.

In my mind, I had *officially* gone over the edge.

***

More than likely, if you have struggled with anxiety, depression, or some other mental illness, you've seen your stress and anxiety levels rise over time. Being aware of those changes can help you take the necessary steps to stay healthy.

DON'T OVERLOOK THE SIGNS

If you ignore the symptoms, you may end up going to the hospital. Even if it doesn't get that bad, you may find yourself unable to function.

It's important to know yourself and notice how your mind and body react to what's happening around you. It's not always bad to feel some stress and anxiety. Those feelings can get us to do something that needs to be done because we're afraid of the consequences if we don't do them. We study for the test because we don't want to fail. We show up for work and do our jobs because we don't want to get fired. We file our taxes even though it can be confusing and time-consuming because we don't want to get fines and penalties later. There are many stressful situations that we just need to face because they are part of life. When we're healthy, we can press on in spite of those anxious feelings.

We can get into trouble when we think we should never feel any stress at all. We're human. Some of us have a higher susceptibility to depression and other mental illnesses, so we may just have to get used to those feelings and ride them out as they come and go. They say nothing lasts forever, and that's certainly true of the emotions that come with mental illness.

Of course, we must be discerning when it comes to our mental health so we don't get into dangerous situations. I'm talking about the times when we're stable and have the ability to make choices about how we're thinking and acting. Sometimes we're too sick to do that and we need to reach out for help.

WATCH FOR THE SIGNALS

If we can gain awareness of the signals our body gives off when we feel stress, we may be able to avoid letting it escalate into something that stops us from functioning. Does your breathing change? Do you feel tightness in your chest? Do you get a headache? Does your eye start to twitch? Figure out where you feel stress in your body.

Try this. Write down what you're feeling. Write down what you're thinking. Getting it all down on paper can help you look at things more objectively and be patient as you either wait for tense feelings to pass or take action to get to better thoughts and feelings.

Let's say you're feeling very stressed and anxious about something happening at your job. You're not able to figure out the new computer program they just implemented and you're just sure your boss is going to fire you if you don't get it figured out quickly. You go to work every day but get further and further behind in your duties because you can't figure out the computer program. You're scared to ask your coworkers or your boss for help because you don't want to appear incompetent.

Work is no longer fun. It's stressful. You put on a good front while you're there, but you're drowning in confusion and despair underneath. At home, you can't relax because you're dreading going back to work and you just know you're going to get fired if you don't figure it out soon.

Your stress and anxiety levels rise. This is going to turn into a full-blown depression if you aren't careful.

When you aren't sick, the solution seems obvious, doesn't it? Talk to your coworkers and get some help so you can figure out the program more quickly and get back to enjoying your job.

But when you're ill, that option doesn't seem as clear. You tell yourself all sorts of things that probably aren't true. "They'll think I'm stupid." "My boss will want to get rid of me and hire someone younger who can do this work better." "I'm not cut out for this." "I shouldn't even have this job."

All that negative thinking will just keep making chemical changes in your brain and make it even harder to think clearly and ask for the help you desperately need.

TAKE ACTION AS SOON AS POSSIBLE

It's important to know yourself and do something helpful or constructive as soon as your stress and anxiety levels begin to rise. You can't let it go on for days and weeks, because the longer it goes on, the harder it will be to get back to a place of clear thinking and a happier state of mind.

The best way to avoid going over the edge is to identify it quickly and take measures to avoid getting close. Noticing your stress level climbing is one of the easiest ways to see that you're wandering into dangerous areas. It's time to look at some things to do to make sure you're staying away from the edge.

Staying Away from the Edge Takeaways

- ⚑ Symptoms can progress until someone is no longer able to function.

- ⚑ Getting help can be stressful, too, but it's worth it.

- ⚑ Try to stay aware of your stress and anxiety levels. They can be good warning signs for you as you stay away from the edge.

- ⚑ Take action as soon as you notice symptoms.

Part 3: Staying Away from the Edge

Chapter 9

Hold Tight to Hope

May the God of hope fill you with all joy and peace as you trust in him, so that you may overflow with hope by the power of the Holy Spirit. (Romans 15:13 NIV)

Okay, so we've gone over the edge, we've looked at how we got there, and now we're hoping to stay far away from it. What can we do to avoid going back there?

The first thing we need to do is hold tight to hope. Choose to fight so you can live. For me, that looks like diving deep into the faith that has been my life ever since I was a little girl. People without faith can hang on when the darkness and despair of their mental illness overtakes them, but I imagine it must be even more difficult for them.

Back at the beginning of this book, I hinted about my faith possibly contributing to my illness. Let's clear that up by exploring it a bit before we consider faith as a possible solution.

Did my faith contribute to my depression? I don't think faith in general leads to depression, but some of the faulty ideas we cling to can exacerbate the symptoms and plunge us deeper into mental illness.

IT'S ALL ABOUT LOVE

Faith in and of itself is all about love—love for God, love for others, and even love for self.

You might disagree, but I am convinced that loving God is the most important thing. I didn't have a problem with that. Reading the Bible and going to church, Sunday school, catechism, and youth group taught me that God is love and that he loves all of us. He loved us so much that he sent his son, Jesus, to die on the cross for our sins. I believed that with all my heart and I wanted to live a life of obedience as a response to that love. When I couldn't do that perfectly, it may have added to the pressures that nudged me toward the edge.

Loving others was a little more difficult, although I seldom showed that on the outside. People considered me a very "nice" girl and I tried to do things that proved that. I felt guilty when I didn't like someone. Sometimes I would be especially nice to them just to relieve that guilt and try to convince myself that I was a good person.

Too often, I felt like a failure in this area. If I couldn't love perfectly then I didn't feel like I was worthy of love from others.

Loving myself? That was the biggest challenge for me. Even though I looked out for my own needs and wants most of the time, there was a problem. I couldn't just enjoy the things I thought I needed and wanted after I got them. No, I had to consider myself selfish for even having those desires. To desire nice things or appreciate God's blessings without sacrifice seemed indulgent. I questioned my worth almost constantly.

If we get confused about any of those things, we could be in danger of getting depressed. *I don't love God enough so I'm a bad person. I feel angry at my spouse/ child too often so I should be ashamed. I hate myself because I'm always messing up.*

Our thoughts—especially when they lean toward the negative—can plunge us into despair and hopelessness. I felt a high amount of pressure when I started the teaching job. I wasn't thinking clearly back then, especially as the weeks went by, but I can dimly recall feeling like I "should" be able to do better, teach better, and feel better just because I was a Christian. I put in my Jenny Simmons CD on the way to school and clung to the words, hoping they would magically take hold and get me to a better place emotionally, but in the meantime, I allowed the negative thoughts to continue running wild in my brain.

WHERE DOES NEGATIVE THINKING FIT IN?

Maybe it's kind of a chicken and egg situation. Do negative thoughts bring on depression or does depression bring on negative thoughts? Whichever one comes first doesn't really matter. Once that spiral gets started and turns to clinical depression, it is nearly impossible to reverse it without medical intervention. That's why it's so important to watch what we're thinking and catch it before it turns into full-scale depression.

I don't really think my faith led to depression. I think it was a combination of hormones (starting in my teens), bad thought habits that took hold over the years, and a lifelong tendency toward perfectionism.

I was so shy and uncertain in my younger years. I had to feel really close to someone before I felt comfortable enough to even talk around them. I rode to and from babysitting jobs without talking to the parent picking me up or dropping me off. I remember riding in the car from Michigan to Illinois for over four hours and not saying one single word to the guy driving us to the Urbana Missions Conference. What must he have thought of me?

I had deep spiritual convictions back then, but lots of pride too. "At least I'm not like so-and-so." (Oh dear, I was a Pharisee!) Well, it's no good to linger back there. Now I'm more like the tax collector: "Lord, be merciful to me, a sinner."[1]

Did something I learned in church make me go to negative places when I succeeded? Pride generally was seen as a bad thing and perhaps even sinful. Couple that with my need to be perfect and I soon felt the need to void out any accomplishments for fear that they could be seen as sinful pride. No one at church really caused me to make that jump, but it's terribly sad how impressionable minds can take words of wisdom to an extreme. There should be a way to teach children that God loves to see them succeed in the things he has called them to do. We all need to be able to avoid the extremes of pride and shame and stay healthy emotionally.

MIXING UP WHAT IT MEANS TO BE "GOOD"

I grew up going to church and Sunday school every single week. I was also a first-born daughter. First-borns are notorious for being perfectionists and people-pleasers. That showed up in my life as I received tons of feedback over the years for how "nice" I was. I was

---

1   The parable of the Pharisee and the tax collector can be found in Luke 18:9–14.

praised for being responsible, caring, smart, thoughtful, hardworking, and lots of other positive adjectives. As I grew older, I believed those adjectives more and more. That's who I was, I thought. I tied those adjectives to who I was as a Christian as well. A good Christian was responsible, caring, smart, thoughtful, hardworking, and everything else.

So when I failed (as we humans do), I felt doubly awful. Instead of just recognizing the shortcoming, I thoroughly believed that I wasn't a good person *and* I wasn't a good Christian.

Is this what my church was teaching? No.

Is this what the Bible said? No.

Is this what I was believing? Definitely. And my mental health suffered because of it.

I knew about God's grace, but I didn't rest in it very often. Occasionally I felt it trying to pour into my life.

In 1999 Gary and I attended a spiritual retreat in Northwest Iowa on separate weekends. We listened to talks by different speakers and participated in special events throughout the weekend that showed us repeatedly how much God loves us and how much grace God shows us. I got it that weekend. At the closing ceremony, I can remember tearfully professing this thought: "I always knew grace was for other people, but this weekend I realized it's for me too." But I went home and promptly forgot (at least most days).

Sometimes I would read a book or lead a Bible study that talked about God's grace and how we couldn't be perfect. We had to "drop our masks" and "be real" with people and live into God's grace. During the study I marveled at God's grace and believed it. But after the study, I would usually go back to my self-condemning, perfectionistic ways.

Those thoughts and habits were deeply ingrained in my brain, and it would take more than just a weekend retreat or a six-week study to change it.

SUICIDAL THOUGHTS

I kept defaulting to the negative whenever I failed. It even got to the point where I had thoughts of suicide go through my mind when I was frustrated with life or disappointed by how I had let someone down. I truly believe that thought had become a coping mechanism (albeit a very bad one) for my stress. I let my mind go there when the pressure got too bad, even though I would never follow through on such a morbid thought (at least I didn't think I would).

Truth is, my mind still goes there sometimes, but I'm finally starting to work on that. Those hopeless thoughts come around much less often, and when they do, it's a warning for me. It's a sign that I have some important work to do to get back to better emotional health.

It's so important to catch the negative thoughts and lies that we tell ourselves as soon as we become aware of them.

We need to pull them out into the light, examine them closely, and change them to get us to better places emotionally.

HOPE COMES IN LOTS OF LITTLE WAYS

When I went to the hospital, I found myself reaching out desperately for the hope I needed. Of course, I had very little hope that weekend, but on Monday Gary brought me a devotional called *Jesus Calling* by Sarah Young. It had a beautiful teal leather cover and the first day I read it, it comforted me. The entry for September 22 said: "Trust me and refuse to worry, for *I am your Strength and Song.* You are feeling wobbly this morning, looking at difficult times looming ahead, measuring them against your own strength."[2]

I certainly was feeling "wobbly" that day in the hospital. Reading that phrase made me cry all over

2   Sarah Young, *Jesus Calling* (Thomas Nelson, 2004), September 22 entry.

again, but it had a tinge of hope in it. God saw me. He knew what I was going through, and he sent just the right thoughts to help me have some hope that things would get better.

Shortly after that, I got a little care package from a friend at church and in it was a brown leather copy of *Jesus Calling*. What a coincidence, and how thoughtful. She also wrote out several Bible verses, inserting my name to personalize them.

I also received a stack of pictures made by the GEMS and Cadets kids (kind of like Christian Girl Scouts and Boy Scouts) at church. I will *never* throw them away. "Robyn is _____" was the theme of the pictures, and the kids filled in the blank with wonderfully encouraging words. "Robyn is caring." "Robyn is beautiful." "Robyn is important." "Robyn is special." "Robyn is a good singer." "Robyn is helpful." Each page was decorated in a special way. Some were plain and simple with just the words and a heart or cross added. Others were colored elaborately, with pictures drawn of me, the church, flowers, and more.

Friends from church and the community mailed cards to the hospital and I pored over every single one. The Scripture verses and poems on the cards were just what my hopeless, despairing heart needed. The words buoyed me up and reassured me that I was loved by my church family, by my friends, and by God.

In the hospital, I read my Bible and soaked in the promises I read there. Promises that God loved me, that he was with me, and that he would stay with me through whatever happened in my life. Gradually I believed he would get me through this time of depression and I would get better.

When anxiety and depression come calling even now, my faith is what I cling to, believing that those feelings will eventually pass and I will feel better again.

When I get busy and don't read the Bible or talk to God, I can see that I'm more likely to fall into those negative thoughts and emotions. When I'm reading the Bible, talking to God, and thinking about my faith, it's easier to stay healthy emotionally.

Feelings will come and go, both negative and positive. No matter which ones are present in my life, I need to make the choice to fight and hold tight to hope. My faith helps me do that.

***

What does it look like to hold tight to hope, whether or not you have faith in God?

I think it probably means focusing on what could happen someday instead of what's happening right now. It's refusing to give up when all the negative emotions are washing over you, choosing to believe that you can and will get back to a better place emotionally.

It's believing medicine will make a difference if your doctor prescribes it.

It's understanding that the counselor will help you process what's going on in your life and things will get better.

It's choosing to fight when your mind and body are telling you to just lie down and give up.

Holding tight to hope will make it easier to do what's needed so you can get healthy and stay that way.

Staying Away from the Edge Takeaways

- ✎ Holding tight to hope is the first step in staying away from the edge.

- ✎ Choose to fight so you can live.

- ✎ True faith is part of the solution for many people.

- ✎ We have to let go of some misconceptions so they don't exacerbate the symptoms of mental illness.

- ✎ Loving God, loving others, and loving ourselves well can help us get better.

- ✎ Watch what you're thinking and catch the negatives before they spiral into depression.

- ✎ God's grace covers all our sins and mistakes. Accepting God's grace will help us live in freedom instead of bouncing between pride and shame.

- ✎ Devotionals like *Jesus Calling* (by Sarah Young), messages from friends, and encouraging Bible verses can help us feel hope during hard times.

- ✎ Holding tight to hope is a decision to believe life will get better with some hard work and the right tools.

Chapter 10

Don't Forget to Take Your Medicine

On each side of the river stood the tree of life, bearing twelve crops of fruit, yielding its fruit every month. And the leaves of the tree are for the healing of the nations.
(Revelation 22:2 NIV)

When I started to get sick during the teaching job, the doctor prescribed an antidepressant for the depression. It took a while to find the right medication and dosage for me. We tried a couple of other drugs but came back to the first one. It was frustrating and unnerving to deal with side effects while I tried different treatments. On one medication I had tremors in my hands and other muscles. On another medicine I had weight gain and not enough improvement over the initial antidepressant, so I went back to what was working. *With* my doctor's knowledge and advice. She had to tweak it a few times before we found the right dose for me. In the hospital it was higher, but later we figured out that I could do well on 10 mg once a day.

The medicine I took played a big role in keeping my brain healthy after I went through that depressive episode. I've always hated taking medications of any kind (I'd wait until my head was about to explode before I'd even take aspirin), but this is one that I decided I must take. Once I got home and settled into normal life, I found that if I missed a couple of days, I could see a big difference in my ability to handle little setbacks and disappointments. With the medicine, I stayed at a more objective, reasonable level. I still cried sometimes when life got overwhelming or I got frustrated with myself or others, but I wasn't crying over minor problems and frustrations anymore.

I continued to take the antidepressant for several years. As I learned more about depression and what I had to do to stay healthy, I eventually reached the point where I wanted to try weaning off the medication. I was on such a low dose, and I didn't like a couple of the minor side effects I experienced. I talked to my doctor and my husband before I tapered off the medicine.

LISTEN TO YOUR DOCTOR

Always follow your doctor's orders, even when you start to feel better and think you can go without your medicine. If you stop suddenly, the shock of withdrawal can worsen your symptoms and lead to complications that might land you back in the hospital. If you've been on a medication for a long time and wonder about discontinuing it, talk to your doctor and develop a plan for weaning off it, checking in with your doctor's office to make sure things are going okay. Make sure your family knows about the change, too, so they can watch out for any problems that might occur.

Time will tell if I ever need to go back on a medication. There are still some times when I feel hopeless and have suicidal ideations, but I had days like that even when I was taking the medicine. I've worked with a counselor on and off over the years, and I'll keep going back as needed so I can get to the root of those disturbing feelings.

I cried more often after I stopped taking the antidepressant, especially at first. I was afraid Gary might insist that I go back on the medication, but he didn't. He acknowledged that I needed to learn how to deal with the normal stresses of life when I found myself crying at times without the medicine in my system. Even now, we keep talking things through, learning together how to deal with the ups and downs of life.

***

FIGHTING THE SHAME

Unfortunately, there is still a stigma attached to mental illness in our society, even though approximately one in four people will deal with some form of mental illness in their lifetime.[1] You may not want to tell everyone you meet that you deal with depression, anxiety, bipolar, or whatever illness affects you, but consider sharing the fact that you take medicine with people that deal with a new diagnosis. Your openness about medications may help someone at the beginning of this journey. Discovering that someone they know takes a medication may give them the courage they need to get help and start a med regimen.

Taking a medication for your mental illness may be necessary, but that won't change some of the possible underlying causes of the depression or anxiety. To get to the bottom of that, you need to start by looking at how you're thinking.

---

1   https://www.who.int/whr/2001/media_centre/press_release/en/

Staying Away from the Edge Takeaways

- It may take some time to find the right medication and dosage for you.

- Always follow your doctor's orders.

- Talk to your doctor and your support system if you want to try weaning off one of your meds.

- Consider telling newly diagnosed people about your experience with medications. They may decide to give meds a try too.

Chapter 11

Get Rid of Negative Thinking

Finally, brothers and sisters, whatever is true,
whatever is noble, whatever is right, whatever is pure,
whatever is lovely, whatever is admirable—if anything
is excellent or praiseworthy—think about such things.
(Philippians 4:8 NIV)

When I started the teaching job, I think I may have been doomed from the very beginning. I felt lots of excitement at first, but once the actual teaching began, I couldn't seem to concentrate on anything but the negative.

I'm not saying I should have ignored the problems and just denied my misgivings. There actually were technology problems to solve, classroom discipline problems that needed to be addressed, and lesson plans to write out each week.

It would have been irresponsible and foolish to just breeze into school each day without a care, laughing off the problems with the computer, ignoring the rising levels of chaos in a few classes, and doing whatever the students felt like doing each day instead of having a plan.

Positive thinking isn't just putting a positive spin on the things that are bothering you and causing you to worry. It's catching the thoughts that are so negative that they make you feel worse and push you toward the emotional edge.

I wonder if I could have continued teaching if I had repeated thoughts like these to myself:

- I can do this!

- I'm a good teacher!

- Many of these students seem to really like Spanish.

- I can ask other teachers for help.

- If I work hard during the week, I can really enjoy my weekend.

- I'm a smart person and I can figure this out, even if it takes a while.

Instead, I was focusing on so many negative thoughts:

- I can't do this!

- I never should have agreed to take this job!

- So many of these kids hate Spanish—it's my fault.

- The other teachers don't seem to be having problems, what's wrong with me?

- I'm a smart person. I should be able to figure this out by myself—but I can't!

- I don't know what to do in my classes tomorrow.

- I can't relax on the weekend because I don't have my grading done or my lessons planned for next week.

- What are the students thinking of me?

- I don't know everything about Spanish.

- The students don't respect me. Why should they?

(It doesn't escape my attention that as I'm writing I was able to come up with only six positive thoughts, but I could rattle off ten negatives. My thinking was definitely skewed!)

THOUGHTS AND FEELINGS ARE CONNECTED

Our thoughts are directly tied to our feelings. If we're thinking useless, negative things about ourselves or our situation, of course we're going to feel uncertain, powerless, frustrated, scared, and other negative emotions.

If, instead, we replace those thoughts with positive ones about ourselves or our situation, we're more likely to feel confident, calm, empowered, ambitious, and hopeful.

If only I had known all this back then! Instead, I thought my feelings came first. *Oh, I'm feeling anxious, so I better not try that. Gee, I feel uncertain, so I'm going to go watch a TV show instead of pushing through to figure out a lesson plan.*

If I had just made a decision—any decision—and gone with it in my lesson plans, it would have been better than what I ended up doing. I sat at the kitchen table or at my desk at school and stared at those blank spaces in the planner book and they paralyzed me. No, *they* didn't paralyze me, *I* paralyzed me, because I was afraid that what I put in those spaces would be the wrong things.

My mind went in circles.

I'd write down that we would do activity X from the online textbook. *Oh, but what if some of the students didn't like activity X? What if we could have better spent our time doing activity Y, or a craft project, or a song? How would the previous Spanish teacher have done it? They probably liked her better than they like me. What can I do to make them like me more?*

If I did fill in the blanks for one day (because I usually did end up just going one day at a time), I would get upset and frustrated if one class got through the plan for the day, but another class didn't get as far because they were messing around and I didn't keep them on task.

As I write this book, all these years later, I can feel a tightness in my chest as I think back to those days. So much anxiety. So much negativity.

DON'T JUST STAND THERE, DO SOMETHING!

In the mornings I started the day with my Spanish 3 class. I would stand in front of the class for the last couple of minutes before the bell rang, not saying much of anything, not relaxed enough to really banter with the kids, just smiling and waiting for the bell to ring. Then I'd go into asking questions to start the class period: "¿Cómo te llamas? (What's your name?) ¿Cómo estás? (How are you?) ¿Qué hiciste este fin de semana? (What did you do this weekend?)"

After several days of this routine, I noticed that some of the girls would come in, put their books on their desks, and then go back out in the hall. I happened to overhear a couple of them talking one day and one said something about not wanting to watch me stand awkwardly at the front of the classroom. I felt embarrassed and even more self-conscious. I made sure after that to just sit at my desk until the bell rang. Negative thoughts piled up in my mind and affected everything I did (or didn't do).

In my mind, it feels like this went on for such a long time, but I have to remind myself that I taught for about a month before I got too sick to teach and went to the hospital. Only a month. Just twenty-eight days for my brain chemistry to become completely messed up by such negative thinking. I have so many regrets about how I was thinking and acting during that month.

DON'T LOOK BACK

We look back too often, regretting mistakes we've made in the past or feeling bad about something we've done. We can look back and wonder about decisions we've made—if they were right or wrong. I know I've done that way too often. I've felt that way about not going to the mission field, about whether I should have gotten married or not (I'm glad I did!), about not going back to the teaching job after I got out of the hospital, and even about taking so much time to write this book. We can drive ourselves absolutely crazy when we live in the past and second-guess every decision we've ever made.

Instead, we need to look to the future, trusting that God has used our past to make us the person he created us to be. That's hard to accept, especially when we've sometimes chosen poorly and experienced the consequences of those choices. And sometimes things have happened to us that we never would have chosen on our own: illness, abuse, accidents, etc. They change the trajectory of our lives in drastic ways, and we're left to live with the end results.

Can we do that? Just live with the results and stop looking back at where it all fell apart? It seems we need to get to that point if we're truly going to live a fulfilling life.

TRY LOOKING AHEAD

Focusing on the past keeps us stuck there. Concentrating on the future will—hopefully—keep us moving in the right direction. Instead of wailing and gnashing our teeth because things didn't go our way, we'll be looking for creative ways to get to where we want to go (and ultimately where God wants us to be).

Before I went to the hospital, I could ruin an entire day just by letting my thoughts run wild and ruminating on something negative that someone said or something I did wrong. Even today, I must really guard against that type of negative thinking. I developed that unhelpful habit over many years of living, so I guess I shouldn't expect immediate results.

On October 20, 2014, I wrote in my journal that I felt happy again and more confident, but I was also wary. I knew I tended to look for some way to feel bad again once I was feeling happy. Over time, I've learned to be more proactive about catching that tendency before it has a chance to ruin my good mood. It's all about how I'm thinking, and I don't allow myself to think the thoughts that lead to feeling bad. (Well, most of the time. There are days, of course, when I fail, but it's easier now to get back to a good place and move on—even without medication.)

I'm learning to catch myself when my thoughts turn negative and I can usually make choices to think in better ways, distract myself with some other activity, or talk it through with a counselor or my husband. It feels good to turn my thoughts around and get them going in a better direction. I'm so happy that I'm improving at getting back to that healthy place!

WE HAVE TO CATCH OUR THOUGHTS

When we let our minds run wherever they want, they will usually go to what we've thought before. No wonder my mind goes so negative most of the time. That's where it's been programmed or allowed to go for more than forty years. (I'm assuming there were some years in there when I was quite young that I was more positive.) We need lots of practice if we hope to keep our thoughts from veering off to the negative.

Here are a couple of problem areas for me. See if you resonate with them, or if you have different thinking issues.

Over the years, I've realized that I'm afraid of anger and feel like it's rejection somehow. It's hard to separate someone's anger from the deep places inside me. That has been a big problem for me in the past, and I'm still working on it in the present. I'm getting better at separating my feelings from what someone else says or does, but it's difficult.

Another thinking problem that occurs way too often for me: I'm scared to fail . . . and I'm scared to succeed. Being afraid of both extremes keeps me stuck in the very middle—living in mediocrity and procrastination. I went on a walk back in October 2014 and asked God about it. I sensed him saying, "You don't trust me," and when I went on to ask how I could trust him more I sensed him saying, "Let things go." I think God was saying that I must let go of control, let go of fear, let go of all the things that keep me stuck in that anxious place of not wanting to go forward. I'm still working on that one too.

Way back then I was already pondering the idea of catching my thoughts. I wrote in my journal: "I think I need to focus on the verse about 'taking every thought captive' because mine run amok way too often and get me into bad places emotionally."

In recent years, I've finally started focusing on that verse (2 Corinthians 10:5) and I'm sharing what I've learned (and continue learning) in a private Facebook group called "Catch Your Thoughts with Robyn Mulder." I also started a podcast with the same name. With help and support, we can all learn to catch our thoughts.

I spent most of my life letting my thoughts run wild. I let negative thoughts push aside all of the positive thoughts I could possibly think, and that left me feeling pretty miserable.

When I made a mistake, I immediately defaulted to "I'm a bad person. I shouldn't ever make a mistake. If I were a better person, I wouldn't have failed like this." I don't know why I thought that way exactly, but it was a terrible habit I got into. If I had successes, I would normally discount them as some kind of fluke. *I got lucky. I wasn't really that great. God just blessed me with success this time, but I didn't deserve it.*

There are so many ways for my thinking to turn negative. And there are so many ways to get my mind going in more positive directions, but I need to take the time to really work on getting it to go that way. It's much more natural to just let the thoughts, feelings, and emotions wash over me, and then I run from whatever is scaring me or making me uncomfortable. I've run in lots of ways: overeating, scrolling Facebook, checking emails when it isn't very important, and watching YouTube videos that are pointless. At times I escape by watching videos or reading info that is good, but

I'm doing it to avoid the discomfort of dealing with the negative emotions that come from completing a difficult task or making a hard decision.

WE HAVE TO WORK AT CHANGING OUR THOUGHTS

It takes a lot of strength to think positively instead of negatively. Our brains get into certain patterns, and it takes a great deal of effort to form new patterns in the way we think.

There's a scene in *Cast Away* where Tom Hanks had to get past the breakers around the island he was stranded on. He would paddle out and attempt to get over the waves, but they would push him back toward the island with so much force. Finally, he found a way to push past them. Once he was free of those breakers, he could continue paddling out to sea where he was finally rescued. He had to exert so much effort to get past that critical spot in the ocean, otherwise he would have continued to be stuck back on the island.[1]

We have to do the same thing with our thinking. We can make small efforts to think in better ways. But then our primitive brains, with all our habitual thoughts and emotions, will push us back to where we've been before.

---

1   I first heard about this concept in a video by language mentor Lýdia Machová (languagementoring.com).

We'll remain stuck in our doubt, hopelessness, despair, uncertainty, and confusion. It will take massive amounts of effort to push past those old thought patterns and get to a place where we can think in new ways and make strides toward living a better life.

What does that massive amount of effort look like practically?

Maybe it looks like writing down our thoughts—every thought—for ten minutes straight. Then we can objectively look at each thought and either accept it or reject it. Chances are, if we're in a depressed mood, most of the thoughts we write down are going to be thoughts we'll be better off rejecting.

Maybe it means planning our day so that we will do something we've been putting off—something we've been afraid to do (so we've remained stuck). We write down that task for a certain time in our planner and when that time comes, we do the thing. We force ourselves to get past the fear, the uncertainty, and the confusion and just do it—not worrying about the outcome, just knowing that pushing past the things holding us back will get us to a better place.

Maybe it means allowing ourselves only a certain amount of time each day to wallow, mope, and cry. This could be a tricky thing, because once the depression has gotten to a certain point we may not be able to control our emotions. But if we're still stable enough emotionally, it might be something to try. Maybe every day from 2:30 to 3:00 is our time for wallowing, moping, and crying. If we feel the urge to do those things at a different time of the day, we can just remind ourselves that we'll do it at 2:30. Maybe we need to write some thoughts down while we're thinking about them. Then, at 2:30, we get out our list, think of all the things stressing us out—all our past hurts and problems, all of our future worries and concerns—and let ourselves wallow, mope, and cry for that half hour. At 3:00, we dry our eyes, rip up our list (or file it away for future reference), and go on with our day—hopefully with a much better mindset and more positive thoughts.

Maybe it means being more deliberate about getting to bed on time and eating more foods that are good for us instead of staying up late and reaching for junk food too often. We can keep a diary of our hours of sleep and what we're eating for a week or so and go over it with the doctor. With help, we can make some changes to improve our physical (and emotional) health.

Maybe it means showing ourselves grace. Grace is the answer to performance anxiety. Grace to live—freely. Grace to live without judgment or the need to produce and perform. Grace to *be* who God wants us to be instead of trying to be who we *think* God wants us to be. (We'll talk about that more in Chapter 15.)

LET GO OF TRYING TO BE PERFECT

Perfection is another thing you must get rid of if you ever hope to live a fulfilling life and thrive with a mental illness. It can show up in your job, your hobbies, your relationships, and any other area of your life. I don't really expect perfection from other people, but I've learned to watch for it in the way I treat myself. When I try to be perfect, I put all kinds of unnecessary pressure on myself and I make myself miserable, even when I succeed at doing something. If I never accept that it's good enough, I can never be satisfied with my accomplishments.

I've worked for many years as a freelance editor for a variety of publishers and authors. One day I got a short booklet to edit for someone. They were pleased with the sample edit I did and hired me. The day I was finishing it up, I felt that familiar twinge of panic threatening to rise. I shoved it down and kept editing, but that evening in the kitchen I started crying in front of Gary and told him how scared I was that I was going to make a mistake. He laughed (I laughed, too, through my tears) because that's a conversation we seem to have every once in a while.

He talked me through it once again, pointing out that I'm just learning to deal with the anxiety that comes up for everyone when they get close to the finish line. When a group of people run a race, there's no pressure for the poor guy in last place. He just has to keep going and finish. But for the people up in front, battling it out for first, second, and third, there's a lot of pressure. "I have to run faster if I'm going to beat that guy!" "I can't let that person catch up with me!" There is anxiety there. Runners just learn to deal with it and push through it to get to the end—and possibly win.

I need to learn to deal with my anxiety too. I need to learn to be more comfortable with the possibility of being wrong or missing something when I edit (realizing that I catch so many mistakes, I'm valuable to anyone who hires me, even if I miss something). Gary also pointed out that we must stay humble. We can't get to the point where we think we don't make mistakes. The fear of making them prompts us to do our best, but we still need to understand that we're not going to achieve perfection.

I've heard all this before. Why is it so hard to live it out? Many speakers talk about "failing forward." We learn from our failures and we move ahead as we learn. I will too. I can't be perfect. Only God is perfect. I need to be a good example of what it means to do my best and humbly apologize when I make a mistake (I'm thinking of editing right now, but it could be in any number of situations).

Perfectionism will definitely push us toward that blasted edge. We might even go over if we ruminate on the impossibility of ever reaching perfection. I need to get comfortable with not being perfect and accept myself as God does—flaws and all.

I do this to myself time after time, and it keeps me from reaching my full potential. Gary even voiced that after we were done with our conversation about my editing (his pep talk and counseling session for me) and settled down on the couch to watch something on TV.

"I wonder what life would be like if you had the self-confidence you should have?" he pondered.

I think I said something smart-alecky like, "I guess we'll never know!"

SOMETIMES THE SIMPLEST THINGS CAN BE OVERWHELMING

One day a few years ago I had an *intense* feeling of hopelessness. It seems silly now, but I'm going to tell you about it so you can see how our thoughts influence our feelings.

Gary's laptop wouldn't print to the church copier and he asked me to take a look at it. I fiddled with it for a long time and nothing worked. *What's wrong with me? I should be able to do this!* Tears dripped down my face and fell onto my shirt. I felt panic starting to well up. As I was clicking, I kept thinking I was going to have to tell Gary I couldn't do it and that he'd have to ask someone else to do it instead.

I felt stupid and worthless and sad and angry—all at the same time. If Gary had come into the office, I'm sure I would have lost it completely and cried harder and gone home very upset. But he didn't come in, and I kept clicking. I decided to search for a new driver online for the copier. I had to find the model number and then found the page where I could download the driver, but it didn't seem like it was working. More tears fell as I thought "I don't know what I'm doing." I must admit, the thought crossed my mind to go home and kill myself. If I couldn't do this task (and I knew there would be many more situations where I would need to do something like this), then I didn't want to live. Of course, I felt horrible for even thinking that, but it was there. No specific plan, but a few possibilities started to come to mind. More tears fell as I clicked and clicked and thought I was messing up Gary's computer even more and I wondered how I would tell him.

But then! All of a sudden, I got one screen telling me something was completed. I wasn't sure what I'd done or how I'd done it, but when I went back to the email and clicked on the attachment and then went to the printer options, the copier was in the list. What a surprise! I clicked to print, and then after a couple of minutes I wiped my eyes and went to the other office to see if it really printed. I plucked the document out of the copier, went back to Gary's office, laid it on his desk, and went home.

So. Negative thinking. Is that all that was happening during my computer/copier dilemma? Why didn't I tell myself, "Gary came to me because he couldn't do it himself" or "He trusts me because I'm always more successful at this stuff than he is." Why was I just letting my mind rush to the darkest place when I got frustrated by the computer not working when I wanted it to? This situation was a reminder that my thinking is of utmost importance. I have to catch my negative thoughts, especially during stressful situations.

The most important thing is to recognize how we're thinking and take steps to change those thoughts if they're not serving us. We need to examine our thoughts and decide if what's going on in our brains is helpful or harmful. Keep the helpful, scrap the harmful.

In my computer situation, the thoughts I was having weren't helping me. They were harmful to such an exaggerated point that I contemplated killing myself just because the computer wasn't cooperating. That's not a healthy way to handle stress!

I'm realizing that how we think is probably one of the most important aspects of maintaining good mental health. When we allow our thoughts to just wander in all directions, we're bound to end up in a negative place. That's what the brain is wired to do.

OUR AMAZING BRAINS

There are basically two parts of our brain. Which part we're using will determine if we respond to life's situations with fight, flight, or freeze, or if we'll choose a more mature, thoughtful response.

Our amygdala (part of the limbic system in our brains) wants to find the negative, the dangerous, the threat, and help us find a way to get back to a safe place. Normally that would mean running, hiding, staying away from all the danger. But life is not meant to be lived in hiding, especially if we are believers in Jesus Christ. He has amazing things for us to do out in his big wide world. Our brains will fight us on everything we want to do unless we're deliberate about combatting negative thoughts and thinking more positive ones instead.

Our frontal lobe (located behind the forehead) can reason things out. It can help us make good decisions and look at situations more objectively. When we're using that part of our brain, we won't just react to something that's happening to us. It takes practice and hard work, but we can learn to think in more helpful ways.

Some people don't have to struggle with it quite as much. They were born with a personality that leans toward optimism, risk taking, and confidence. Others must make a greater effort to think positively and work toward better mental health.

When someone is in the deepest pit of despair because their brain chemistry is messed up, it can be nearly impossible to choose to think more positive thoughts. The brain gets stuck in a loop of negativity. "This will never end." "It's hopeless." "I'm no good." "Why do I always mess up?" (And then your brain will try to answer that question by showing you all the ways you've messed up in the past and it will throw out possible reasons for those failures.)

OUR BRAINS NEED HELP

When a person is at that place emotionally, they need someone or something to help them get started on the path to better mental health. A doctor may prescribe an antidepressant or another medicine to help with anxiety or other symptoms. Remember, those medicines take time, and they may need to be tweaked several times before you and your doctor find something that works for you. A counselor may need to help you voice the thoughts that are keeping you stuck in that pit of despair. Hopefully, they can help you see the error of certain thoughts and how they are keeping you from enjoying life and accomplishing all you want to do.

It can feel safe to stay in bed all day, but that doesn't accomplish much. It just leads to more negative thoughts. "I'm so lazy." "Why can't I get anything done?" "What's wrong with me?"

Taking a close look at what you're thinking will get you moving in the right direction, help you find more purpose in life, and get that spiral rising in an upward direction—to health—instead of spinning downward deeper and deeper into depression.

If you can figure out how to change your negative thinking to more positive thoughts, that's great. But sometimes those thoughts are so complicated, or we've thought them for so long, we need help to look at them more objectively and work through them.

You just might need a good counselor to help you turn them around.

Staying Away from the Edge Takeaways

- 🦋 Our thoughts are directly tied to our feelings.

- 🦋 We need to be realistic, but we also need to catch negative thoughts and replace them with something more positive.

- 🦋 Negative thoughts can get us into a downward spiral. Unfortunately, our brains can become addicted to this type of thinking. It gets harder and harder to get our thoughts going in a positive direction instead.

- 🦋 Looking back with regret isn't helpful. Focusing on the future will get us to healthier places.

- 🦋 We must exert massive amounts of effort if we want to form new thought patterns.

- 🦋 Your brain will try to keep you safe, but it can also help you face your fears and grow emotionally.

Chapter 12

Seek Wise Counseling

*The way of fools seems right to them,
but the wise listen to advice. (Proverbs 12:15 NIV)*

My eyes followed my counselor's hand as she moved it back and forth repeatedly. I wasn't sure what I was really supposed to be doing. She had told me that EMDR (Eye Movement Desensitization and Reprocessing) was a new method that could help my mind get unblocked from memories that were keeping my brain from moving toward healing.

"Focus on my hand," she urged. I tried, but I felt absolutely nothing and couldn't see the point in continuing.

"I think I want to stop," I said.

"No, let's keep going."

I strained to focus and do what she asked, but my mind was bouncing through all sorts of possibilities. This wasn't working. Suddenly, I started to chuckle.

She stopped. "What are you thinking right now?" she asked.

"I thought you kept doing EMDR to force me to be more assertive."

She seemed a bit confused and said that she hadn't been doing that, but she honored my request to stop. I guess I wasn't ready for a new method yet.

***

Counseling is a helpful way to change our thinking and develop better ways to interact with our world and stay emotionally healthy.

I've gone to counseling several times in my life.

When we lived in Rock Rapids, Iowa, I went to see our pastor during that year when I was angry with my children and worried about how I was feeling and acting. He said some helpful things, but he also made the bizarre comment that I would make a good counselor someday. I was flattered, but also frustrated. How could I be a good counselor when I was feeling such anger toward my kids and wondering about my sanity? That was not helpful, and I wished he hadn't said it.

Later, when we lived in Orange City, Iowa, I went to see another pastor. Pretty much the same thing happened. He gave me some helpful advice, but just spent one session with me and assured me that it would be okay. He didn't have the training to really go into deeper issues and ongoing counseling.

These men meant well, but they just weren't trained to provide counseling for someone who was dealing with depression. The first *official* time I had counseling was when we lived in Holland, Michigan and Gary was in seminary. I had read that I could get free counseling through the seminary and so I held on until we got to Holland, even though I was struggling with depression in Orange City as we got closer to the move. As I mentioned before, I had gotten a prescription for an antidepressant from my doctor when I was pregnant with Dylan, but I never took it because I was afraid of what it might do to the baby.

Once we got to seminary, I had a couple of sessions with the professor of counseling, and he gave me good advice. He started to delve into some of the issues I was struggling with and had me read a book or two. He recommended a counselor in Holland and I went to see her for a while. She was helpful. I finally started to work on some of my negative thinking and figure out where some of my false beliefs came from. She's the one who tried the EMDR session with me. I felt bad that it didn't work, sure I had failed somehow.

THIS MIGHT BE A CONTROL PROBLEM

Looking back on it now, I think that another one of my issues is that I don't like to lose control. I think to have EMDR really work you must let your mind go and allow thoughts to come as they will. That's scary for me. I want to be aware of what I'm thinking, analyze whether it's right or wrong thinking, and never be out of control. Those are good goals to have most of the time, but at times they hinder me. I find it hard to just relax and let things happen however they're going to happen. I'm constantly considering whether I'm doing things right, if I could be doing things better, or if someone else is doing things right (although that doesn't bother me as much as whether *I'm* doing things right). I guess that's something I probably need to keep exploring with a counselor.

Gary graduated from seminary and we interviewed at several churches before finding his first call. I don't think I ever saw a counselor during the five years we lived in Minnesota, although I definitely went through times of depression and the ups and downs that came with it.

I saw a Christian counselor for a while after we moved to eastern Iowa. (Evidently moving brings out some intense feelings in me that take a little help to work through.) I learned so much from this counselor and tried to practice the good ways of thinking that would help me deal with life. I stopped seeing her when she cut down on her hours and I thought I was fine for a long time.

Later, I saw a counselor a couple of times for some stress I was having, and after that I went for quite a while without needing to talk to someone. Then the teaching job came along and I completely lost sight of hope. When I got out of the hospital, I had regular appointments with my psychiatrist (for medications) and my counselor (for talk therapy).

THOUGHTS CAN BECOME HABITS

Counselors can help you search for flaws in your thinking patterns, especially those caused by habits cemented in place over many years. Science shows that our brains develop actual pathways that our thoughts follow. We'll default to those habitual ways of thinking, particularly when we experience certain triggers. It takes conscious effort and hard work to develop new ways of thinking and create new pathways that are healthier for our minds, but it is possible. The ability of the brain to form new neural pathways is called *neuroplasticity*.[1]

---

1   Find out more about neuroplasticity at https://www. verywellmind.com/what-is-brain-plasticity-2794886

It takes conscious effort and sometimes an objective third party to help us develop new ways of thinking when we get into certain situations or hear certain words.

I know myself much better now than I did in my younger years. Sometimes that helps me to think differently about certain situations, but sometimes I'm too lazy or tired to fight negative feelings and I fall into the same unhealthy patterns and emotions.

LETTING GO OF PERFECT

I think my biggest problem is perfectionism. I usually feel very good about myself when I'm doing everything right and succeeding. When I fail myself or others, I can feel very down. I can see that I've improved over the years in this area. I used to get very, very upset when I made a mistake or made someone mad or disappointed. I cried and felt like I wasn't worth much of anything. I still hate to disappoint people, and I try not to do it, but I usually can look at the situation objectively and I'm not as self-critical. I realize the mistake I've made, apologize when necessary, and determine to try to do my best in the future, realizing that I'll never be perfect.

***

If you deal with anxiety, depression, or some other mental illness, consider seeing a good counselor that can help you stay on track and objectively point out if you're starting to go toward the edge again.

It's important to pick the right person when you go for counseling. If you don't feel comfortable with your counselor, then you won't be honest with that person and you'll be less likely to make progress. I asked one of my counselors for her opinion on this topic, and she graciously wrote something up for me. Here's a great quote from Jennifer Schneiderman, LISW at the University of Northern Iowa:

> Working with a counselor may not be for everyone, and each person's treatment should be individualized. Research tells us that the most effective approach is the combination of therapy and medication. Having a positive relationship with one's mental health therapist is the most essential pathway to a good outcome.

CONSIDER SEEING A CHRISTIAN COUNSELOR

If you are a Christian, seeing a Christian counselor makes so much sense. That person will be able to remind you of what the Bible says as the two of you look at how you're thinking. There are counselors who advertise as Christian, while others (especially those who work in hospitals or clinics and don't have their own private practice) can't talk about their faith openly, but they are able to talk about it during your counseling sessions if you bring it up and talk about how faith fits in with your treatment.

I've had both types. Some were explicitly Christian and brought the Bible and faith into all aspects of the counseling. Others were in a secular setting, but they were able to respect my faith and talk about it in context as we worked on my thoughts and my mental health.

WHAT TYPE OF THERAPY IS BEST?

Most counselors specialize in certain types of therapy, so it might be helpful to summarize some of the most common types here. If one sounds like it might work, you can look for a therapist with that kind of training. We don't have the space to go into tons of details about each option, but you can search for resources online if you want to dive a little deeper into something that sounds interesting.

Cognitive behavioral therapy (CBT) is a common type of talk therapy. You can work with a counselor in a structured way and become more aware of your inaccurate or negative ways of thinking. CBT can help you view challenging situations more clearly and respond to them in more effective ways.[2]

———————

2   https://www.mayoclinic.org/tests-procedures/cognitive-behavioral-therapy/about/pac-20384610

Attachment-based therapy is a brief, process-oriented form of counseling. It looks at the connection between an infant's early attachment experiences with primary caregivers, usually with parents, and the infant's ability to develop normally and ultimately form healthy emotional and physical relationships as an adult.[3] Knowing which attachment style you have can be helpful as you work with a counselor and develop healthier ways of relating to the people in your life.

Dialectical behavior therapy (DBT) is a modified type of CBT. Its main goals are to teach people how to live in the moment, develop healthy ways to cope with stress, regulate their emotions, and improve their relationships with others.[4]

EMDR (Eye Movement Desensitization and Reprocessing) is an interactive psychotherapy technique used to relieve psychological distress.[5] You can essentially relive traumatic experiences while your attention is diverted by the movements of the therapist. This allows you to be exposed to the thoughts or memories without having such a strong psychological

3   https://www.psychologytoday.com/us/therapy-types/attachment-based-therapy

4   https://www.verywellmind.com/dialectical-behavior-therapy-1067402

5   https://www.healthline.com/health/emdr-therapy

response. It is especially useful in treating things like PTSD and trauma.

Exposure therapy is a type of cognitive behavioral therapy that is most frequently used to treat obsessive-compulsive disorder, post-traumatic stress disorder, and phobias. The patient works with a therapist to identify the triggers of their anxiety or rituals. Then they can be exposed to those triggers in a controlled environment with the goal of being able to cope with them more effectively.[6]

Interpersonal psychotherapy (IPT) helps people with depression address current concerns and improve interpersonal relationships. Therapists might utilize various techniques, such as role-playing, to help people in therapy adjust how they relate to their world.[7]

Mentalization-based therapy (MBT) is a kind of psychotherapy that engages and exercises the important skill called mentalizing. It can help people consciously perceive and understand their own feelings and thoughts.

---

6   https://www.goodtherapy.org/learn-about-therapy/types/exposure-therapy

7   https://www.goodtherapy.org/learn-about-therapy/types/interpersonal-psychotherapy

MBT is less structured than therapies like CBT and is usually done more long-term.[8]

Psychodynamic therapy focuses on the psychological roots of emotional suffering. Its hallmarks are self-reflection and self-examination.[9] Research is also showing that this type of therapy may lead to ongoing changes, even after therapy has ended.

Electroconvulsive therapy (ECT) is sometimes used as a last resort in cases where someone's mental illness is severe and doesn't respond to other forms of treatment. It involves a brief electrical stimulation of the brain while the patient is under anesthesia.[10] After ECT, most people need some form of maintenance treatment—psychotherapy, medication, or possibly ongoing ECT treatments.

How's that for a smorgasbord of therapy options! You can read more about each vein of therapy at the links provided in the footnotes or some of the books included in the List of Resources. Knowing the methods used and the focus of each type of therapy can help you choose

---

8   https://www.goodtherapy.org/learn-about-therapy/types/mentalization-based-therapy

9   https://www.apa.org/news/press/releases/2010/01/psychodynamic-therapy

10 https://www.psychiatry.org/patients-families/ect

the counselor who could best help you with your specific mental illness.

In this book we're looking mostly at anxiety and depression, because that's what I've experienced. Cognitive behavioral therapy (CBT) may be enough to treat most forms of those illnesses (although other types of therapy may also be effective). If you've been diagnosed with a more complex illness—like bipolar or schizophrenia—you may need to talk with your doctor about which therapy could be most helpful for you.

As for me, I've been learning that the way I think really influences how I feel. I've been learning and practicing new ways of thinking ever since my major depressive episode. I even started a private Facebook group and a podcast called *Catch Your Thoughts with Robyn Mulder*. As I've already mentioned, the inspiration for that came from the phrase "We take captive every thought to make it obedient to Christ" in 2 Corinthians 10:5.

Most of the counselors I've seen over the years have used cognitive behavioral therapy (CBT). Learning to choose more helpful thoughts can be one of the tools that keeps us away from the edge.

CATCH YOUR DISTORTED THOUGHTS

Here are some unhelpful thinking styles[11] (list taken from psychologytools.com, but I wrote the thought examples).

All-or-nothing thinking – Thinking in extremes. It's black-and-white thinking. Something is perceived as either 100% good or 100% bad. *I never do anything right.*

Catastrophizing – Jumping to the worst possible conclusion. *I'm ten minutes late so my boss is going to fire me.*

Over-generalizing – Seeing a pattern based upon a single event or being overly broad in the conclusions we draw. *Nothing good ever happens to me.*

Mental filter – Only paying attention to certain types of evidence. *I got a raise, but that doesn't count. In my performance review, my boss told me I had to work on being more assertive. I don't deserve a raise!*

Disqualifying the positive – Discounting positive information or twisting a positive into a negative. *She complimented me, but I'm sure she was just trying to be nice.*

Jumping to conclusions – Mind reading or predicting the future. *He didn't say hi so he must hate me!*

_____

11   https://www.psychologytools.com/self-help/thoughts-in-cbt/

Low frustration tolerance – Saying things like "This is too difficult," "This is unbearable," or "I can't stand it." *I'm never going to get the hang of this new job. It's too hard!*

Minimization – Discounting the importance of something. *It's not that big of a deal.*

Emotional reasoning – Assuming that because we feel a certain way our hunch must be true. *I feel embarrassed so I must be stupid.*

Demands – Using words like "should," "must," and "ought." *I should be able to handle this situation better.*

Labeling – Assigning labels to ourselves or others. *I'm a loser. They're such an idiot.*

Personalization – Taking too much or too little responsibility. *This is all my fault.*

Of course, there is some overlap in this list. Certain thoughts could fall under more than one type of unhealthy thinking. As you look over this list, can you see any that have become habits for you? I've gotten stuck in every single one of them at some point in my life. We can learn and practice healthier ways of thinking, but we may always need to be on guard against these unhealthy habits. Once our brains are used to thinking in certain ways, we will default to those ways of thinking, just like a river flows down the path it has carved out in the land. It takes a great amount of pressure to force a river into a new place, and it takes an extraordinary amount of work to get our thoughts running in new neural pathways in our brains. They're going to want to go in the same familiar ruts they've gone through in the past, but it's worth the effort to help our brains form new pathways. With time and lots of practice, we'll begin to think in more positive ways without as much effort. When our brain tries to default to that old pathway, it will only take a little mental nudge to get it back into the new groove. We'll feel better as a result of the hard work we put into forming those new pathways, especially with the help of a counselor or support group.

A GOOD COUNSELOR CAN HELP YOU EXAMINE YOUR THINKING

Regular appointments with a counselor can help you change unhealthy thought patterns like these and make sure you're thinking in right ways. Of course, as a Christian, I would recommend seeing a Christian counselor so the therapy helps you live out and rely on what you believe the Bible says, but if you aren't a believer, there are many excellent counselors who don't bring faith into their practice.

Whichever counselor you choose, it's important to be honest with that person. If you hold back what you're thinking and only let them see the "good" things you're thinking, you'll never attain the skills you need to have when those negative thoughts and feelings try to take over.

Finding a good counselor may take a few tries. They should be good at helping you analyze your thoughts, not just telling you what to do to feel better. After all, they can't be with you all the time. You're going to have to learn to catch any negative, unhelpful thoughts you're having on your own and turn them around so you can move forward. Once you've done that, you're on the way to better mental health.

Joining a support group can help cement those new thought patterns into that amazing brain of yours.

Staying Away from the Edge Takeaways

- Intense feelings can be a sign that you need to work with a counselor for a while.

- Counselors can help identify flaws in your patterns of thinking.

- Neuroplasticity means your brain is able to change and form new neural pathways.

- A good counselor can help you stay away from the edge. Make sure it's someone you connect with so you're more likely to make progress.

- If you are a believer, a Christian counselor may be helpful, but don't be afraid to see someone who isn't listed as a Christian. A good counselor will allow you to explore how faith affects your mental health.

- Research different types of therapy and choose one that seems like it might be helpful.

- With some work, we can change our unhelpful thinking styles.

Chapter 13

Make Sure You Have Support

Two are better than one, because they have a good return for their labor: If either of them falls down, one can help the other up. But pity anyone who falls and has no one to help them up. (Ecclesiastes 4:9–10 NIV)

Jessica[1] blinked back tears as she told us about her week. "There's one salesman who always acts so impatient when I'm trying to fill his orders. He makes me feel so stupid and then I get more nervous and I start messing up! I just dread it whenever I hear him on the phone." Jessica was still getting used to her new job in a call center. She had shared that she cried on the way home from work almost every single day.

The rest of us nodded sympathetically. Then one guy burst out, "You should make a Bingo card!"

"Uh, what?"

---

1   Name and other details changed to protect privacy.

"Yeah," he went on excitedly, "You could have a card with all of the possible situations that could come up during your shift. 'Said good morning instead of good afternoon.' 'Salesman didn't say thanks.' 'Accidentally disconnected someone.' 'Ordered the wrong part number.' 'Jerry the Jerk called.' BINGO!"

Jessica and the rest of us burst into laughter. It was a crazy idea, but it got her mind off the immediate problem and helped her see it in a lighter way.

The support of people who understood how she felt was helping Jessica cope with a hard situation.

***

WHO'S IN CHARGE?

So, whose responsibility is it to help someone stay well if there is a mental health diagnosis? Is it the doctor's responsibility? A spouse's? The patient's? Ideally, all of those would be working together to make sure someone stays healthy.

Ultimately, the person with the diagnosis will need to call on others to help and support them. Someone with a physical injury or illness often needs to get help from a doctor or specialist; a person with a mental illness will need help from a professional at some point if they really want to get better. Sure, they can limp along in life, dealing with their symptoms, functioning well sometimes and not functioning well at other times. To really get to a place where they thrive will probably mean they have to invite mental health professionals into the process to evaluate and treat them (with medicines, talk therapy, or maybe both).

When someone has surgery, they usually need someone to stay with them for a time so they can get help with the things they aren't able to do (like dressing themselves, cooking a meal, cleaning, bathing, and other tasks). This is understood and even expected by people in the recovery community. They don't say, "Why don't they just do it themselves?"

When someone comes home from the mental health unit of a hospital, they usually don't ask for someone to stay with them. If that person has a spouse, then they have someone there, but the ill person is often expected to jump right back into their normal routine. This is understandable (mostly because mental illness isn't as visible as other health problems), but someone suffering with mental illness often *can't* jump right back in (nor should they). Compassionate family members will try to give their loved one time to heal before expecting them to fully resume their everyday responsibilities.

What about single people who have a severe mental health crisis that lands them in the hospital? What happens to them when they go home? They are alone with their thoughts and feelings, maybe still fighting the debilitating symptoms of the mental illness and sometimes they can't cope yet. They need support too. It's difficult, because many people don't want to admit they've had a mental health crisis. People in their social circles may not even know that anything happened.

As Christians, we need to reach out when we know someone is going through a time of crisis emotionally. We could offer to bring a meal, clean their house, or just sit and be with them while they recover from the crisis.

If only we could get more comfortable talking about our emotional health. We might get better at asking for help. We might get better at offering help. We all need support. We can't do this all on our own, as much as we would like to.

FRESH HOPE PROVIDES HOPE AND SUPPORT

One of the most helpful things for keeping me away from the edge is my Fresh Hope[2] support group. I first found out about Fresh Hope through my friend Koreen. We had been friends and neighbors many years before, but our most recent move had brought us back to within a half hour of each other. She had her own struggles with mental

2   Find a group near you and check out their online resources at http://freshhope.us.

illness over the years. When she heard that I had gone to the hospital, she reached out and we started texting about our feelings and experiences. We got together for lunch occasionally and found it helpful to support each other. We have different triggers, symptoms, and strategies for staying well, but it helps so much to be able to talk to a friend who knows what you're going through. We read the book *Fresh Hope* by Brad Hoefs and then went through training together to become facilitators of our own Fresh Hope groups.

After we got it started, our little Fresh Hope group met a need every week for me. Often there were only three or four of us at the meeting, but we all found it helpful to talk things out, learn together, and remind each other that people know what it's like to deal with a mental health diagnosis and we could encourage each other to keep "pushing through."

We started Fresh Hope groups in both of the churches we went on to serve later. We met twice a month, seeing a small group of people who came regularly and some people who came once and then didn't join us again. That's okay. It's good that people know groups like Fresh Hope exist and they can turn to them if they're struggling. Also, many individuals have contacted me personally even though the stigma they feel still prevents them from attending.

Sometimes we watch a video about mental health on YouTube, sometimes we talk about an article, sometimes we pick a topic card from the pack provided by Fresh Hope and discuss the questions, sometimes we just sit and talk about what is going on in our lives and how we are managing the pressures of life. It all works.

Fresh Hope was started by Pastor Brad Hoefs in Nebraska. He suffered his first bipolar episode in 1995. After a relapse in 2002, he knew he needed to attend a support group, but he was frustrated with the groups he attended. It seemed like they just focused on managing the symptoms of the disease and he ended up feeling even more depressed after attending. He collaborated with his psychiatrist to come up with the seven tenets that are used in Fresh Hope support groups today. Now he's active with Fresh Hope and reminds people: "I *am not* bipolar. I *have* bipolar."

People with a mental health diagnosis can attend, as well as their loved ones (but they don't have to attend together—it's fine if someone attends alone). After a time to check in, the group goes through the seven tenets. Each principle has a section for those with a diagnosis, another for loved ones, and a third that applies to the whole group. The tenets remind everyone involved that there are choices to make. Those with a diagnosis have to keep choosing to "push through" and work with their doctors and other support people to stay healthy. Loved ones need to find that balance between letting their friend or relative wallow in their symptoms and pushing them too hard. Everyone involved works together to help all of us live healthier, more fulfilling lives and thrive in spite of a mental health diagnosis.

Fresh Hope is an excellent resource for those who have a mental health diagnosis and/or their loved ones. The important thing is that people know there is a place they can go and share what they are going through. Finding people who have had similar experiences brings so much help and healing.

Fresh Hope is unique in that it is peer-led and Christian. They make no apologies about bringing Bible verses into the discussion and one is listed after each tenet. As a Christian, those verses remind me where my hope comes from and point me to answers to my problems. We have had people attend who don't believe in God, but they still find plenty to encourage and inspire them in the weekly discussions. Fresh Hope also has online groups available for those who can't get to an in-person group.

***

ASSEMBLE YOUR OWN PERSONAL SUPPORT GROUP

Besides an official support group like Fresh Hope, it is vital that those of us with a mental health diagnosis surround ourselves with a personal support group.

The pain of mental illness pushes us to isolate ourselves. It is imperative that we avoid doing that. When we distance ourselves from others, we are much more likely to go over the edge. When we isolate, we can convince ourselves that nobody loves us, nobody cares, nobody needs us.

It's true, life can be painful at times. Relationships can be messy, frustrating, and complex. But they can also bring joy and make life worth living. Social connections are often where we find help and hope and healing.

For me, I tend to want to isolate when I'm feeling the slightest bit down. I don't want to go to church or Bible study or out for coffee or to some other event I put on my schedule. I would rather stay at home and avoid talking to others. I'm almost always glad after I force myself to go out to the activity I'm tempted to skip, but it's a big deal to choose to go instead of staying in my little cocoon.

We must make sure we're not trying to endure this alone. That's an almost certain pathway toward the edge.

Having a supportive network will allow the people we trust to help us by pointing out the signs that show we're in danger and heading toward the edge again. They can notice symptoms we'd rather ignore. They can step in when we're teetering and about to go over. The more people we have supporting us, the more likely it is we'll be able to stay away from the edge and live a more healthy, happy, and fulfilling life.

Our personal support group can include our spouse, children, close friends, our family doctor, psychiatrist, counselor, pastor, or an online support group. The key is to have people in our lives that we feel comfortable talking to with complete honesty, knowing they'll help us if they can see that we're starting to go toward the edge again. We don't need people that will allow us to wallow in our sadness or make excuses for our behavior. Neither do we want people who will bully us when they don't like how we're acting. We need supportive people who will show us unconditional love and also speak those hard truths when they see us making poor choices regarding our mental health.

We need people who understand what it's like to deal with a mental illness—either from personal experience or because they've studied mental health extensively.

We may need to educate our family members and friends so they best know how to help us. We need to be honest with them and tell them how we're feeling, even when things are bad. When we find ourselves thinking suicidal thoughts, we must speak up so we can get help and not go over the edge.

Trusting and communicating with our personal support group will be one of the best ways to stay healthy emotionally and stay far away from the edge.

Staying Away from the Edge Takeaways

- 🔥 You will need to call on others to help and support you.

- 🔥 Mental illness isn't as visible as a physical illness, but the patient still may need time away from their normal routine while they heal.

- 🔥 We need to get more comfortable talking about our mental health.

- 🔥 Fresh Hope support groups can be a vital tool for those with a diagnosis and/or their loved ones. (Check out freshhope.us for more information.)

- 🔥 We all need a personal support group that includes family members, friends, doctors, pastors, and mental health professionals.

- 🔥 Relationships can be messy, but they can also bring joy and make life worth living.

- 🔥 Isolation can add to our depressive or anxious symptoms.

Chapter 14

Sitting with Others

When Job's three friends . . . heard about all the troubles that had come upon him, they set out from their homes and met together by agreement to go and sympathize with him and comfort him. When they saw him from a distance, they could hardly recognize him; they began to weep aloud, and they tore their robes and sprinkled dust on their heads. Then they sat on the ground with him for seven days and seven nights. No one said a word to him, because they saw how great his suffering was. (Job 2:11–13 NIV)

It's hard to be understanding of people who are in the depths of depression when you're not there yourself. Even when you've been there in the past (like I have), it's sometimes hard to feel compassion.

I don't like to admit that. I mean, it seems like since I felt bad enough to want to kill myself and I could hardly function, I should be able to sympathize with people who talk about feeling so bad that they can't do the dishes, can't fold the laundry, can't get out of bed, can't take care of their kids, can't go to work, and all of the other things they can't do because they're depressed.

As I am right now, I know in my head that they can't help it, but a part of me wants to say, "Just do x, y, and z and you'll feel better soon."

It's tough to find the balance between these two extremes: "Do this and you'll get better" and "It's okay if you never get better because you can't help it."

Depression and anxiety happen. We don't know what has happened externally and internally to the people in our lives to result in this mental illness. We need wisdom and discernment to know when we need to push ourselves and others to work hard to get out of a bad emotional state. Sometimes that's effective and hard work brings improvement.

SOMETIMES YOU JUST NEED A BREAK

And sometimes a person just needs time to rest. If we have a mental illness, we can give ourselves permission to take a break, rest, and recover before we jump back into life. If we are a loved one for someone with a mental health diagnosis, we can determine to just sit and be with our spouse, child, sibling, or friend. Loving them with no pressure to "snap out of it" can help them feel a little bit better, and after they've rested, they may feel ready to take some next steps to get to better emotional health.

Each situation and person is going to be different, but we can choose to sit together when life is too hard, pray together when all hope is gone, and work together to get to a better emotional state—one that will make sure we stay away from the edge. In the Bible, Job's friends did well when they sat with him after all of his losses. It wasn't until they opened their mouths that their counsel became unuseful.

Do you have friends who will sit with you? It takes honesty and vulnerability to find those people in your life. Often, we need to take the first step, but then we can be wonderfully blessed with others who understand what we're going through and are willing to listen when we're ready to talk.

Staying Away from the Edge Takeaways

- Sometimes it's hard to find compassion for someone with a mental illness (including ourselves!).

- We need wisdom and discernment to know when to push ourselves to work hard and when to rest when it comes to our mental health.

- Sometimes the best thing we can do is sit with someone who is going through a hard time emotionally.

Chapter 15

Living Into Grace

"My grace is sufficient for you, for my power is made perfect in weakness." Therefore I will boast all the more gladly about my weaknesses, so that Christ's power may rest on me.
(2 Corinthians 12:9 NIV)

As we were wrapping up our Fresh Hope meeting recently, I felt good about the discussion we'd had. The short video had suggested several ways to combat the harmful anxiety that can paralyze us and keep us from living well. Six members had shown up and I felt grateful for the support we could show each other.

Then Gary ruined it all.

"I bet you've been feeling anxiety about misspelling *anxiety*, haven't you?" he teased.

I laughed along with everyone else as he pointed out the typo on the handout I had prepared to go along with our video. I hadn't noticed it during the meeting, which added to my embarrassment. I'm a freelance editor, after all. I'm proud of how good I am at catching misspelled words, punctuation errors, and other mistakes.

"I noticed it, but I decided not to say anything," one friend said.

"What's everybody laughing about?" another member asked. I think I may have blushed a tiny bit as I had to point out the word "anxity" on the second-to-last line of the sheet in his hand.

When Gary and I got home, I had to talk about it a little more. I mentioned how much I hated it that I had missed that typo.

Gary chuckled. "I never would have brought it up if I had known it was going to bother you so much. I just thought you had been sitting there worrying about it through the whole meeting."

Looks like I still have some work to do when it comes to living into grace.

***

This is the last chapter I find myself working on as I finish up *Staying Away from the Edge*. I'm afraid it's going to be the hardest one to write because I'm still learning how to do this. At 57 years old, you'd think I'd have this all figured out by now. After all, I've been a Christian almost all my life and I've certainly read my Bible, listened to many sermons, and gone through various studies that talked about what it means to accept God's grace.

GRACE AND THE GOSPEL

I learned as a little girl that all of us are sinners. God is a perfect God and he can't allow any sin into heaven. Our sin separates us from God.

Is that hard to read? Do you want to protest? Maybe you're thinking *I'm not that bad!* I suppose all of us want to compare ourselves to other people, and maybe we come out looking pretty good when we list off all of the sins other people commit. But the truth is, *all* of us sin. Anything that misses the mark of God's perfection condemns us.

But there's good news (that's what the word *gospel* means)! God had a plan to restore us. He sent his Son Jesus to live a perfect life here on earth. He suffered a cruel death on a Roman cross and he was buried in a tomb, but he didn't stay there. On the third day, the tomb was empty and Jesus appeared to his disciples and many others. He rose!

After forty days, he ascended into heaven, and he's still there. He reigns with God the Father and the Holy Spirit.

If we believe that and accept Jesus as our Lord and Savior, we can be sure we'll go to heaven when we die someday. Jesus' blood covered our sins and made us righteous. That's grace!

We don't have to earn it or do something to "pay Jesus back." We just have to accept his grace and live into it.

I've accepted it. It's the living into it that trips me up some days.

THINGS THAT HOLD US BACK

In other chapters of this book, I've shown you that I have a tendency to be a perfectionist, a procrastinator, and an idealist. All of those things can try to nudge grace aside and cause me to doubt my worth.

Here are some of the things I think when I'm not living into grace:

- I should have this figured out by now. I'll never get it right!

- Why would God love me? I keep messing up!

- I'm such a bad example for my kids. Why can't I do things better?

- I always wait until the last minute to get things done. If I were a better person I'd plan things out ahead of time and get things done early.

- If I can't do this perfectly, then I might as well not even do it at all.

- What's the use? I'm never going to improve!

I hope you recognize most of those thoughts as distortions (we talked about those in Chapter 12). Thinking that way will never let me live well. I'll always be beating myself up when I fail. I'll forever be analyzing every move I make, measuring my progress against where I *think* I should be.

THERE'S A BETTER WAY

There's a better way to think—a better way to *live*. Living into grace will allow us to live with confidence and peace. We'll be able to show compassion to ourselves and others.

Like I said, I'm still practicing this. I have a long way to go, but I'm learning. I've often joked that I do things the hard way (especially when Gary asks me why I'm doing something a certain way). I don't know why I've thought I had to make things more difficult, but I'm finally getting tired of that. I can see the benefits of working smarter, not harder. I don't want to make life harder than it has to be—for me or anyone else.

Maybe I can finally start enjoying life instead of picking every decision apart to see if it was the "right" one. Maybe I can do something for fun and not feel stress in the back of my mind because I think I should be doing something more productive instead. Maybe I can be grateful for the days when I don't experience the symptoms of depression and anxiety. I don't have to wonder when those feelings will come back, I can just move forward, thankful for the reprieve from my illness. Maybe I can live into grace.

I must be making some progress because I've noticed a couple of surprising victories in my thinking lately.

THE STOP THAT DIDN'T STOP ME

One day I headed for home after my swim workout at our local university (I'm not a student, but I use the pool at their wellness center). After I turned onto the highway, I was surprised to see flashing red and blue lights in my rearview mirror. I checked the speedometer and I wasn't going over 55, so I was thoroughly confused, but I pulled over and waited for the officer to come to my window.

"Ma'am, Stadium Road is only 25 miles per hour," he stated. This was campus police for the university and

I had been pushing it a bit on the previous road as I was leaving the campus. I hadn't done it intentionally, but I *was* speeding.

After checking my license and other papers, he told me he was just going to give me a verbal warning this time. Whew! No ticket. I was so relieved. I thanked him and promised to watch my speed in the future.

I consider that a victory because in the past I probably would have been crying and beating myself up all the way home after that traffic stop. This time I listened to the warning and I moved on with my life. I was a bit embarrassed about getting stopped, but I didn't turn it into a reason to doubt my worth. I didn't even cry!

PUSHING PAST MY EXCUSES

Another area where I've seen significant improvement is doing things even when I don't feel like it. In the past I would have listened to the excuses in my head about why I shouldn't have to do something. *I'm too tired. It's such a pain to get ready to go. I probably won't enjoy it. I'm too busy. I have so much to do here at home.*

This has applied to little things I have to do around the house, but it has also been evident when I push myself to do my swimming workouts. Many times, I start to talk myself out of going, but I can usually push past it and get it done. (Sometimes I have a little extra encouragement from Gary. That helps.) I gather my suit and towel in the morning and stick my backpack near the door. I put on my coat and grab my keys. I drive to the wellness center. I walk in and trudge up to the locker room. (Through all of this my brain is still trying to convince me to forget it and go back home.) I put my suit on, stretch my swim cap onto my head, and grab my goggles and towel. Then I scurry through the cold hallway to the pool. (I'm still not looking forward to getting in.) I grab a kickboard and make my way over to the lanes, telling the lifeguard hello as I pass her chair.

Now comes the moment of truth. I sit on the edge and swing my legs a few times before I finally ease in and go underwater. I did it! There's no going back now. That first push off the wall feels so good, and my workout begins. There are moments of out-of-breath panting and feeling my heart beat out of my chest, but for the most part it feels good. I'm *always* glad I decided to go to the pool (even though I really think I could skip it every time).

Pushing through my negative thoughts about exercise is another victory for me. I'm doing hard things instead of taking the easy way out.

I suppose that's part of living into grace. I don't get to just coast through life, doing whatever I want to do. I'm learning to choose thoughts, activities, and challenges that make me a stronger person—physically, emotionally, and spiritually.

LIVING INTO GRACE WHEN IT COMES TO MENTAL HEALTH

We've been talking about lots of different ways to stay away from the edge when it comes to mental illness. There are things we can do to get healthy and stay healthy emotionally. But we also have to live into grace, not expecting perfection when we consider our symptoms.

You might be feeling fine for a long time, but then one day your depression rears its ugly head and you can barely function. Living into grace might look like refusing to believe that you'll never feel good again.

You allow yourself to feel the emotions that come over you during that difficult period, and then you bravely take whatever steps are necessary to get yourself away from the edge. You show yourself compassion, but you also determine to fight to get back to a healthy mindset. You might not "feel" like going to the counselor, or taking your meds, or attending the support group, but you know you'll feel better once you do those things. So you do them. And on the days you can't, you hang on tight to hope and try again the next day.

That's living into grace, allowing God's grace to flood over us and sustain us despite our feelings, experiences, or accomplishments (or lack of them).

Staying Away from the Edge Takeaways

- It will probably take a lifetime to fully learn how to live into grace.

- The gospel (the good news) is that Jesus died so we can have a relationship with God.

- Lots of thoughts and attitudes hold us back.

- There's a better way to live.

- If you practice and keep trying, you'll see improvements.

- We can't expect perfection when it comes to mental health—we have to live into grace.

As We Keep Going

*The steadfast love of the LORD never ceases; his mercies
never come to an end; they are new every morning; great is your
faithfulness. 'The LORD is my portion,' says my soul, 'therefore
I will hope in him.'"
(Lamentations 3:22–24 NIV)*

Now that I'm almost ten years past my episode of major depression, I'm feeling pretty good most of the time. Some days it's hard to even remember the worst feelings. I asked Gary about it once, and he told me I had been *really* sick. "You said there was no hope, that there was nothing good in life."

When he mentioned that, I did remember how hopeless I felt. It was terrible. I would sit in front of my empty lesson plan book and page through the teacher's edition of the textbook or click through the previous teacher's lesson plans online and just think, "I can't do this!"

As I was working on the early drafts of this book, one of my editors pointed out that I tended to want to blame someone for the depression I went through. Especially myself. "I worked myself into a depression after just a month of teaching" is what I wrote at first. Thanks to her observation, I was able to change the parts of this book that attempted to affix the blame to someone or something.

It's human nature, I suppose, to want to blame someone when something goes wrong. When we get depressed, we want to figure out who to blame. It can't be our own fault, can it? It's his fault. It's her fault. It's the situation's fault. It feels better to get the responsibility off of ourselves.

What if it's nobody's fault?

What if it's just a perfect storm of a series of difficult life circumstances, a lack of good coping skills, and brain chemistry that gets all messed up?

We need to resist the urge to blame anyone for our anxiety or depression (especially ourselves). Sometimes it just happens. The important thing is to reach out for help. Anxiety and depression are highly treatable illnesses, and with the right combination of medicine, therapy, and coping skills, you can get back to a healthy life.

KEEP IT BETWEEN THE LINES

When I was a kid, I can remember riding my bike down our street and being scared when I saw that someone had taken the time to edge their lawn. The lawn looked beautiful, but that little groove next to the sidewalk was just wide enough for a bike tire to sink in and make me wipe out.

You know, thinking back on it now, I don't think I ever did fall over, but there were times when I got too close, my tire went in, and I had a moment of panic before I could fight my way back onto the sidewalk again.

I preferred the lawns that weren't edged. The grass butted right up against the sidewalk and spilled over onto the pavement. If I got careless about where I was riding, I noticed the grass and easily steered back to where I should be.

Maybe that can be a reassuring thought as we deal with our mental health. Very rarely is the line between health and illness clearly marked out. We can begin to wander into unhealthy thought patterns and behaviors at times. It takes awareness to notice that we're not on the main path and diligence to do whatever it takes to get back on track.

Compare that with driving a car. In flat areas or places with shallow ditches, there is no guardrail. If someone goes off the road, the consequences are minimal. When the terrain gets more extreme, you may find some sort of barrier along the roadway. Sometimes there is just a cable strung up between posts to mark the side of the road. Other times there is a thick metal guardrail that helps keep cars on the highway. You'll see concrete barriers on the interstate, stopping vehicles from veering into oncoming traffic. You can tell how dangerous a place is by the strength of the barrier.

Usually.

In some places, there are so many deep ditches and drop-offs that it would be impossible to add barriers to every mile of the highway. In those places, drivers must be especially careful and remain in control of their car so they can get to their destination safely.

We have to do the same with our mental health.

WATCH FOR THE SIGNS

Sometimes we'll see warning signs. An author may include a trigger warning at the beginning of an article or book and we decide if we can or can't handle that piece. We may get teary in a situation that wouldn't normally upset us, so we know that it's time to take a look at our mental health and see what we need to do to take care of ourselves. A flash of anger may warn us to take a break before we blow up at someone.

Occasionally, something will happen that brings back some of the strong feelings of anxiety and hopelessness I felt back in 2014. It's terrifying, but it's also strangely reassuring.

I remember how sick I was back then. I think about the things I've learned about myself and mental illness in the years since that time. I know I can make choices that will get me back to good mental health. I never have to get that sick again. But when I do start that downward spiral, God is right there with me, and I'll get through it with his help.

I'm praying this book can help others who are going through experiences like mine. As we all learn to take action so we can stay away from the edge, maybe the world will become a place where everyone is emotionally healthy. Can you imagine that?

AN EMOTIONALLY HEALTHY WORLD

I can picture it, but it looks so different from what we see now. I think a world where we're all healthier emotionally will look like people being honest about how they're feeling. It will look like people asking for help when they're emotionally wounded. It will look like people catching their thoughts and turning them around instead of ruminating for days, weeks, months, and years about the same worries and problems. We will see a dramatic drop in the number of suicides because people will know how they're feeling, and they'll reach out for help instead of going over the edge. It will look like people being more understanding and kind because they will think about how their words affect someone else. Maybe there will be a lot less rejection and loneliness. People will succeed and accomplish great things because they will learn how to push past their fear of failure, and they'll reach their goals.

What a wonderful world that would be.

WE HAVE TO BE HONEST AS WE KEEP GOING

I wish I could end this book with a glowing report about how I've left depression and anxiety in my past because I learned to hold tight to hope, took meds when I needed them, got rid of negative thinking, sought wise counseling, and joined a support group.

The truth is, I still struggle.

The tempting thing to do is just sit in one place and let the world go by. There's safety there, knowing what to expect and not risking the negative things that could happen if we try something new.

Maybe that's why it has taken so long to write this book. I've known that people are struggling. I've heard people's hard stories. I've wanted to help others who have become mentally ill, but the prideful part of me wanted to make sure I had overcome this problem before I told my story and offered my advice—so everyone else could overcome it too.

Please forgive me for my idealistic thinking and waiting so long to get this book into your hands. I now know that staying away from the edge is an ongoing process rather than a one-time achievement.

I suppose I could have written ten different books in the years since my major depressive episode. And I could probably write ten more in the years to come.

I'm not the woman I was when I had to go to the hospital. I'm not the woman I'll (hopefully) be in the future. I have to be content with what I've written right now, praying it will help someone else stay away from the edge.

Sometimes, God does completely heal someone who suffers from anxiety or a mental illness, and that's a wonderful thing. More often, he promises to be with someone who suffers in that way, asking them to trust him through all the emotional pain and turmoil that anxiety and mental illness cause.

THE END (ALMOST)

So, I end this book with some promises and some questions.

First, I promise to do everything I possibly can to stay away from the edge.

I'll hang on to hope when everything inside me says there's no hope left. *"Those who hope in the L*ORD *will renew their strength. They will soar on wings like eagles; they will run and not grow weary, they will walk and not be faint" (Isaiah 40:31 NIV).*

If I start to spiral down into depression again, I will swallow my pride and get back on a medication so I can think more rationally and get better.

I will keep learning to catch my negative thinking and turn it around so I can feel better and thrive in life, instead of wallowing in negative thoughts and staying stuck.

I will talk to a counselor when I need help getting my thinking going in the right direction again.

I will keep attending Fresh Hope, surrounding myself with people who understand what it's like to live with depression and anxiety so we can help each other choose hope.

In the years ahead, I know I'll have good days and I'll have bad days. No matter how terrible the bad days feel, I promise not to give up.

Now, some questions for you:

Will you promise to do everything you possibly can to stay away from the edge?

Will you hold tight to hope?

Will you take your meds (if they're part of your treatment plan)?

Will you get rid of negative thinking?

Will you seek wise counseling?

Will you join a support group?

Will you promise not to give up, no matter how hard it gets?

I pray you can answer each of those questions with a resounding *yes*. If you do, you're much more likely to stay away from the edge and enjoy the usually wonderful, sometimes frustrating, often exciting, some days difficult, occasionally boring, generally satisfying, and ultimately worthwhile life you're living.

Let's all keep going and, even more importantly, stay away from the edge!

List of Resources

In today's world, we have an overwhelming number
of resources available to us at the click of a button
on our computers. Thankfully, more and more people
are realizing that people have a need for help when
they deal with mental illnesses like depression and
anxiety. I'm listing some possibilities for you, with
the understanding that more resources will become
available in the months and years ahead. Explore what's
out there and take advantage of anything that can help
you stay away from the edge.

Books:

I Love Jesus, But I Want to Die: Finding Hope in the Darkness of Depression by Sarah J. Robinson (WaterBrook 2021). This beautiful book will help many people who deal with the frustrating reality of being a Christian who still struggles with the dark thoughts that come with a mental illness.

Maybe You Should Talk to Someone by Lori Gottlieb (Houghton Mifflin Harcourt 2019). This best-selling memoir gives readers a glimpse into talk therapy from both sides of the couch. Gottlieb is a therapist who ends up going to see a therapist. Reviewers call it funny, touching, and transformative.

Beyond the Storm: How to Thrive in Life's Toughest Seasons by Debra B. Morton (Thomas Nelson 2019). While ministering to victims of Hurricane Katrina and grieving the death of her granddaughter, Morton realized that the key to pushing forward in the midst of setbacks was having a defined set of coping skills. She developed a "Storm Playbook" which teaches people how to go on after devastating circumstances in life.

The Upward Spiral by Alex Korb (New Harbinger Publications 2015). An excellent book, full of the science behind mental illness, but also humorous and helpful for turning the downward spiral around and becoming more healthy emotionally.

Feeling Good: The New Mood Therapy by David D. Burns (Harper 2008, reprint edition). First written in 1980, *Feeling Good* is considered one of the best books ever written about cognitive behavioral therapy (CBT). It offers strategies for changing the thoughts that lead to feelings of depression.

Unshakable Hope by Max Lucado (Thomas Nelson 2018). At first glance, this does not look like a book about depression, but the first chapter touches on the despair and hopelessness in today's society. The book does explore the hope believers can have because of God's promises. Chapter 11, "Joy Is Soon Coming," covers the topic of suicide, but the rest of the book paints a broader picture of how Christians can find hope in the middle of a shaky world.

An Unquiet Mind: A Memoir of Moods and Madness by Kay Redfield Jamison (Vintage 1996). This is a memoir about one woman's experience with bipolar disorder.

Furiously Happy: A Funny Book About Horrible Things by Jenny Lawson (Flatiron Books 2015). The author of this book decided to fight back against depression and anxiety by blogging about being "furiously happy" and making a choice to really live life. I laughed out loud many times during this collection of essays, but it's not for everyone. Obscenities and questionable topics occur throughout (the author warns readers in her disclaimers at the beginning).

Broken (In the Best Possible Way) by Jenny Lawson (Henry Holt and Co. 2021). Another release by Jenny Lawson, the author continues to share her experiences with depression in her hilarious and touching style.

Mind Over Mood by Dennis Greenberger and Christine A. Padesky (The Guilford Press 2nd edition 2016). Like *Feeling Good,* this book also helps sufferers of depression and other disorders through cognitive therapy. The twelve chapters teach about our moods and what we can do to change them, but they also include quizzes and exercises to help apply the concepts being taught.

The Happiness Trap by Russ Harris (Trumpeter 2008). This book introduces acceptance and commitment therapy (ACT) to help readers overcome their stress and anxiety and improve the quality of their lives. Its short chapters explore many different ways to practice ACT.

Depression, Anxiety, and Other Things We Don't Want to Talk About by Ryan Casey Waller (Nelson Books 2021). This pastor, therapist, and co-sufferer shows that mental health issues are not a symptom of a spiritual failing or insufficient faith. Suffering is the very thing our Savior seeks to heal.

Companions in the Darkness by Diana Gruver (InterVarsity Press 2020). The author reassures readers that they are not alone if they struggle with a mental illness. She introduces them to seven saints who also dealt with the darkness of depression and doubt.

Praise the Lord and Pass the Prozac: A Hopeful, Helpful, Humorous Devotional by James Watkins and Faith A. Watkins (Hope & Humor 2022). James has written humorous devotions based on ten affirmations for those dealing with mental health issues. His daughter has added applications as a therapist.

You Are Not Alone: The NAMI Guide to Navigating Mental Health by Ken Duckworth, MD (Zando 2022). This is NAMI's first book— an essential resource for individuals and families seeking expert guidance on diagnosis, treatment, and recovery. It's full of advice from experts and wisdom from real people and families.

Podcasts:

It seems like many podcasts are here today and gone tomorrow, but I'm listing a few that are available at the time of this writing. You can use your favorite search engine to explore all of the options related to mental health. Use your own discretion when you decide what to listen to. If a podcast makes you feel worse or is just plain confusing, it might be time to find something new.

Catch Your Thoughts with Robyn Mulder. Yes, I have a
    podcast. Tune in to find help and inspiration as you
    catch the negative thoughts that may be contributing
    to your depression or anxiety. You can also join
    the free, private Facebook group of the same name
    and connect with other people who want to learn to
    think better and stay away from the edge.

Feeling Good. David Burns wrote the book *Feeling
    Good* in 1980. Since then, the book has undergone
    several revisions, and this podcast was started in
    2016. It is geared toward therapists who use CBT
    in their practices, but those dealing with depression
    and anxiety can glean principles to help them in
    their own journeys toward better mental health.

The Anxiety Chicks. Alison Seponara (a licensed
    therapist) and her co-host Taylor Marac (a registered
    dietician) explore all things anxiety healing while

keeping it real. They often talk about their own struggles with mental health as they share tools and strategies needed to heal the anxious mind.

Therapy in a Nutshell. This isn't a podcast, but
please check out the YouTube channel of Emma
McAdams. Her free videos are always helpful
and informative, and she has a variety of different
courses you can take to help with different aspects
of mental health. She also has free resources at her
website: therapyinanutshell.com.

Music:

I created a Spotify playlist ("Staying Away from the Edge") with some of my favorite songs for hanging on during times of depression. They won't take away your mental illness, but they might make it a little easier to endure the symptoms. I'm including the list here, along with a little explanation of why I love each song.

Truth Be Told (Matthew West) I always think of two
teenage girls I know when I hear this on the radio.
It's a song that was special to them as they dealt
with their own experiences of depression. If we're
honest, we can encourage and support each other
through all of life's ups and downs.

What Faith's About (Jenny Simmons) This is one of the
songs I blasted on my way to school each day. It

didn't pull me out of the depression, but I still love it for the hopeful message it provides.

5 Minutes at a Time (Superchick) I love Superchick, but I didn't discover this song until recently. Perfect timing, and it's a great song to remind us that we need to keep moving forward. Never give up!

Hold On (Wilson Phillips) I know this song was originally written with substance abuse in mind, but I always think of someone dealing with depression when I hear it. Hold on for one more day!

Faithfully (TobyMac) TobyMac lost his oldest son to an accidental drug overdose in 2019. This song reminds us of the goodness of God, even when we're in dark times.

One More (Superchick) This song is on my MP3 player, and it always helps me do another lap of the pool when it comes on. Even when we feel overwhelmed or exhausted, with God's help we can "go one more."

The Becoming (Jenny Simmons) Another song from the album I listened to every morning on the way to my teaching job. We need to hang on during times of depression so we don't miss the beauty of becoming.

Magic Wand (Chris Rice) I pulled a few of these songs from an old mixtape I made for myself. I labeled it "Depression Busters." This song reminds us that we can't wave a magic wand and have our problems disappear. Progress comes from simple choices we make every day.

My Heart Is a Stone (Michele Pillar) Another "depression buster" song, this one tells us that God is chipping away at the hard parts of our hearts. The Holy Spirit rearranges things and we end up getting new hearts. We're going to be okay.

Thank God I Do (Lauren Daigle) Released in 2023, I recently discovered this song. I absolutely love this line: "I don't know who I'd be if I didn't know You, I'd probably fall off the edge."

I'm Up (Michael W. Smith) This upbeat song reminds us that Christians are free and saved. We can be "up," even when times are hard.

Firm Foundation (He Won't) (Cody Carnes) This one reminds me of a youth event we attended with a group of teens in Colorado in 2023. Imagine a couple thousand teenagers with hands raised high, singing along as the band leads them in worship. "He's never let me down. He's faithful through generations, so why would He fail now? He won't!"

Organizations:

There are many groups that work to help people dealing with mental illness. Here are some to check out, but you can also do an online search and find organizations that cater to your age group or your specific illness.

Fresh Hope (freshhope.us) provides Christian, peer-led support groups for those who want to thrive in spite of a mental health diagnosis and/or their loved ones. Their website has information about finding or starting a group, as well as links to their blog and podcast.

NAMI (National Alliance on Mental Illness - nami.org) envisions a world where all people affected by mental illness live healthy, fulfilling lives supported by a community that cares. Their website is full of information and resources that can help those living with mental illness.

APA (American Psychiatric Association – psychiatry.org/patients-families) is the professional organization for psychiatrists, but it has devoted an entire section of its website to patients and their families. You can find brief definitions of major mental health disorders, basic information about mental health, and a blog with useful articles about many topics related to mental health.

Bring Change to Mind (BC2M – bringchange2mind.
  org) wants to end the stigma and discrimination
  surrounding mental illness. Their website includes
  shared stories, a blog, videos of people opening up
  about their life with mental illness, and suggestions
  for what to say (and not to say) to people
  experiencing mental health challenges.

Related Bible Verses

Mental illness is not a spiritual problem, but growing stronger in your faith might help as you work with your doctor and other professionals. You can't just read the Bible and pray your way to better health, but faith can be one of the essential components of getting healthy emotionally. Here are some verses* (related to the chapters in Part 3) to inspire and encourage you as you stay away from the edge. I hope they'll whet your appetite for more of God's wisdom as you seek to live well (even with a mental health diagnosis).

*(All verses taken from the NIV)

Chapter 9: Hold Tight to Hope

Romans 15:13 - May the God of hope fill you with all joy and peace as you trust in him, so that you may overflow with hope by the power of the Holy Spirit.

Isaiah 40:30–31 - Even youths grow tired and weary, and young men stumble and fall; but those who hope in the LORD will renew their strength. They will soar on wings like eagles; they will run and not grow weary, they will walk and not be faint.

Jeremiah 29:11–13 - "For I know the plans I have for you," declares the LORD, "plans to prosper you and not to harm you, plans to give you hope and a future. Then you will call on me and come and pray to me, and I will listen to you. You will seek me and find me when you seek me with all your heart."

2 Corinthians 4:16–18 - Therefore we do not lose heart. Though outwardly we are wasting away, yet inwardly we are being renewed day by day. For our light and momentary troubles are achieving for us an eternal glory that far outweighs them all. So we fix our eyes not on what is seen, but on what is unseen, since what is seen is temporary, but what is unseen is eternal.

Psalm 27:13–14 - I remain confident of this: I will see the goodness of the LORD in the land of the living.

Wait for the LORD; be strong and take heart and wait for the LORD.

Chapter 10: Don't Forget to Take Your Medicine

Proverbs 17:22 - A cheerful heart is good medicine, but a crushed spirit dries up the bones.

Ezekiel 47:12 – "Fruit trees of all kinds will grow on both banks of the river. Their leaves will not wither, nor will their fruit fail. Every month they will bear fruit, because the water from the sanctuary flows to them. Their fruit will serve for food and their leaves for healing."

Matthew 9:12 - Jesus said, "It is not the healthy who need a doctor, but the sick."

1 Corinthians 6:19–20 - Do you not know that your bodies are temples of the Holy Spirit, who is in you, whom you have received from God? You are not your own; you were bought at a price. Therefore honor God with your bodies.

3 John 1:2 - Dear friend, I pray that you may enjoy good health and that all may go well with you, even as your soul is getting along well.

Psalm 147:3 – [The LORD] heals the brokenhearted and binds up their wounds.

Chapter 11: Get Rid of Negative Thinking

2 Corinthians 10:5 - We demolish arguments and every pretension that sets itself up against the knowledge of God, and we take captive every thought to make it obedient to Christ.

Philippians 4:8 - Finally, brothers and sisters, whatever is true, whatever is noble, whatever is right, whatever is pure, whatever is lovely, whatever is admirable—if anything is excellent or praiseworthy—think about such things.

Romans 12:2 - Do not conform to the pattern of this world, but be transformed by the renewing of your mind. Then you will be able to test and approve what God's will is—his good, pleasing and perfect will.

Philippians 4:6–7 - Do not be anxious about anything, but in every situation, by prayer and petition, with thanksgiving, present your requests to God. And the peace of God, which transcends all understanding, will guard your hearts and your minds in Christ Jesus.

Proverbs 3:3–6 - Let love and faithfulness never leave you; bind them around your neck, write them on the tablet of your heart. Then you will win favor and a good name in the sight of God and man. Trust in the LORD with all your heart and lean not on your own understanding; in all your ways submit to him, and he will make your paths straight.

Chapter 12: Seek Wise Counseling

Proverbs 20:5 - The purposes of a person's heart are deep waters, but one who has insight draws them out.

Psalm 32:8 - I will instruct you and teach you in the way you should go; I will counsel you with my loving eye on you.

Proverbs 12:15 - The way of fools seems right to them, but the wise listen to advice.

Proverbs 19:20 - Listen to advice and accept discipline, and at the end you will be counted among the wise.

Chapter 13: Make Sure You Have Support

John 15:12 - My command is this: Love each other as I have loved you.

James 5:16 - Therefore confess your sins to each other and pray for each other so that you may be healed. The prayer of a righteous person is powerful and effective.

Romans 15:14 - I myself am convinced, my brothers and sisters, that you yourselves are full of goodness, filled with knowledge and competent to instruct one another.

Galatians 6:2 - Carry each other's burdens, and in this way you will fulfill the law of Christ.

Acts 20:35 - "In everything I did, I showed you that by this kind of hard work we must help the weak, remembering the words the Lord Jesus himself said: 'It is more blessed to give than to receive.'"

Chapter 14: Sitting with Others

2 Corinthians 1:3–4 - Praise be to the God and Father of our Lord Jesus Christ, the Father of compassion and the God of all comfort, who comforts us in all our troubles, so that we can comfort those in any trouble with the comfort we ourselves receive from God.

1 Thessalonians 5:11 - Therefore encourage one another and build each other up, just as in fact you are doing.

Romans 12:15 - Rejoice with those who rejoice; mourn with those who mourn.

Job 2:13 - Then [his friends] sat on the ground with [Job] for seven days and seven nights. No one said a word to him, because they saw how great his suffering was.

1 Peter 4:8–10 - Above all, love each other deeply, because love covers over a multitude of sins. Offer hospitality to one another without grumbling. Each of you should use whatever gift you have received to

serve others, as faithful stewards of God's grace in its various forms.

Chapter 15: Living Into Grace

Ephesians 2:8–9 - For it is by grace you have been saved, through faith—and this is not from yourselves, it is the gift of God—not by works, so that no one can boast.

Matthew 11:28–30 - [Jesus says:] "Come to me, all you who are weary and burdened, and I will give you rest. Take my yoke upon you and learn from me, for I am gentle and humble in heart, and you will find rest for your souls. For my yoke is easy and my burden is light."

Romans 5:20–21 - The law was brought in so that the trespass might increase. But where sin increased, grace increased all the more, so that, just as sin reigned in death, so also grace might reign through righteousness to bring eternal life through Jesus Christ our Lord.

2 Corinthians 12:9–10 - "My grace is sufficient for you, for my power is made perfect in weakness." Therefore I will boast all the more gladly about my weaknesses, so that Christ's power may rest on me. That is why, for Christ's sake, I delight in weaknesses, in insults, in hardships, in persecutions, in difficulties. For when I am weak, then I am strong.

Hebrews 4:15–16 - For we do not have a high priest who is unable to empathize with our weaknesses, but we have one who has been tempted in every way, just as we are—yet he did not sin. Let us then approach God's throne of grace with confidence, so that we may receive mercy and find grace to help us in our time of need.

About the Author

Robyn Mulder grew up in Wyoming, Michigan (a suburb of Grand Rapids). A happy childhood somehow evolved into problems with depression and anxiety once she got to high school and college. A major depressive episode in 2014 sent her to the hospital, and ever since then she's been on a journey to maintain her emotional health. Some days are good, and some days are hard, but she'll never give up. Besides this book, she also shares her thoughts at her blog at robynmulder.com and in her podcast: *Catch Your Thoughts with Robyn Mulder* (along with the free, private Facebook group of the same name).

She and Gary live in South Dakota. Gary is a pastor and Robyn writes and does freelance editing. Their four children—Erin (married to Ayden), Allison, Blake, and Dylan—all conveniently decided to live in Lincoln, Nebraska (at least for now). Robyn and Gary love going down to visit, especially now that they have a cute grandson named Halston and an adorable granddaughter named Clarke.